# HIDING FOR OUR LIVES

## Esther's Story

*Followed by the same events as remembered
by Ezjel Lederman, her husband
and Bogdan Zal, their rescuer.*

Written by Esther Lederman

Copyright © 2007

ESTHER LEDERMAN

Library of Congress
ISBN # 1-4196-8002-1

Printed in the U.S.
Booksurge Publishing
www.Booksurge.com

*Dedicated to my children, grandchildren, the memory of my husband Ezjel, and to Bogdan Zal and his family who saved our lives.*

*This book was originally a gift from my children for my 75th birthday. My husband and my own typewritten accounts of the events of WWII were transformed into a coherent transcript. A limited quantity of the book was printed in 2004. I decided to reprint the book because so many people wanted to read it.*

*I want to thank my daughter, Ruth Sack, who was the force behind the publication of our stories. Without her energy, talent and ability to coordinate the process, which involved organizing two manuscripts, designing the book and cover, dealing with printers and publishers, etc, this book would never have come into being. She also engaged the capable help of our editor, Leslie Virostek. Thank you, Ruth.*

## TABLE OF CONTENTS

Preface to Esther's Story . . . . . . . . . . . . . . . . . . . . . . . . . . . . . . .1

A Happy Childhood . . . . . . . . . . . . . . . . . . . . . . . . . . . . . . . . . . .2

Distant Rumblings of Trouble . . . . . . . . . . . . . . . . . . . . . . . . . . .6

The Summer of '39 . . . . . . . . . . . . . . . . . . . . . . . . . . . . . . . . .12

German Invasion . . . . . . . . . . . . . . . . . . . . . . . . . . . . . . . . . . .15

Flight from Lodz . . . . . . . . . . . . . . . . . . . . . . . . . . . . . . . . . . .21

Life in Kielce . . . . . . . . . . . . . . . . . . . . . . . . . . . . . . . . . . . . .24

Chmielnik . . . . . . . . . . . . . . . . . . . . . . . . . . . . . . . . . . . . . . . .27

A Young Couple in Love . . . . . . . . . . . . . . . . . . . . . . . . . . . . . .33

Rumors of Atrocities . . . . . . . . . . . . . . . . . . . . . . . . . . . . . . . .37

Other Departures . . . . . . . . . . . . . . . . . . . . . . . . . . . . . . . . . . .43

A Solo Journey . . . . . . . . . . . . . . . . . . . . . . . . . . . . . . . . . . . .45

The Beginning of Confinement . . . . . . . . . . . . . . . . . . . . . . . . .56

Our Unpredictable Protector . . . . . . . . . . . . . . . . . . . . . . . . . .59

From the Attic to the Pantry . . . . . . . . . . . . . . . . . . . . . . . . . . .62

Imminent Dangers . . . . . . . . . . . . . . . . . . . . . . . . . . . . . . . . . .69

Liberation . . . . . . . . . . . . . . . . . . . . . . . . . . . . . . . . . . . . . . . .73

An Odyssey to Freedom Begins . . . . . . . . . . . . . . . . . . . . . . . .79

Laboring as Free People . . . . . . . . . . . . . . . . . . . . . . . . . . . . . .85

Lodz Revisited . . . . . . . . . . . . . . . . . . . . . . . . . . . . . . . . . . . .90

A Reunion . . . . . . . . . . . . . . . . . . . . . . . . . . . . . . . . . . . . . . . .94

The Journey Continues . . . . . . . . . . . . . . . . . . . . . . . . . . . . . .98

The Baby Arrives . . . . . . . . . . . . . . . . . . . . . . . . . . . . . . . . . .106

In America . . . . . . . . . . . . . . . . . . . . . . . . . . . . . . . . . . . . . . .115

Photos . . . . . . . . . . . . . . . . . . . . . . . . . . . . . . . . . . . . . . . . . .116

Bogdan's Story . . . . . . . . . . . . . . . . . . . . . . . . . . . . . . . . . . . .120

Preface to Ezjel's Story . . . . . . . . . . . . . . . . . . . . . . . . . . . . . .130

The History that Set the Stage . . . . . . . . . . . . . . . . . . . . . . . . .131

A Portrait of Chmielmik . . . . . . . . . . . . . . . . . . . . . . . . . . . . . .134

Life as a Jewish Boy . . . . . . . . . . . . . . . . . . . . . . . . . . . . . . . . .137

Hitler's Push . . . . . . . . . . . . . . . . . . . . . . . . . . . . . . . . . . . . . . .142

The Germans Arrive . . . . . . . . . . . . . . . . . . . . . . . . . . . . . . . . .145

Gradual Deterioration, and the Formation of the Ghetto . . . . . . .150

Young People Coping with Daily Life . . . . . . . . . . . . . . . . . . . .153

Assistance from the Zals . . . . . . . . . . . . . . . . . . . . . . . . . . . . . .156

Five in Hiding . . . . . . . . . . . . . . . . . . . . . . . . . . . . . . . . . . . . .161

The Bunker . . . . . . . . . . . . . . . . . . . . . . . . . . . . . . . . . . . . . . .165

The Russians Arrive . . . . . . . . . . . . . . . . . . . . . . . . . . . . . . . . .171

Lublin . . . . . . . . . . . . . . . . . . . . . . . . . . . . . . . . . . . . . . . . . . .176

Lodz and Chmielnik Revisited . . . . . . . . . . . . . . . . . . . . . . . . .182

Out of Poland . . . . . . . . . . . . . . . . . . . . . . . . . . . . . . . . . . . . .186

A Stay at Neu Freimann . . . . . . . . . . . . . . . . . . . . . . . . . . . . . .190

Getting to the U.S. . . . . . . . . . . . . . . . . . . . . . . . . . . . . . . . . . .196

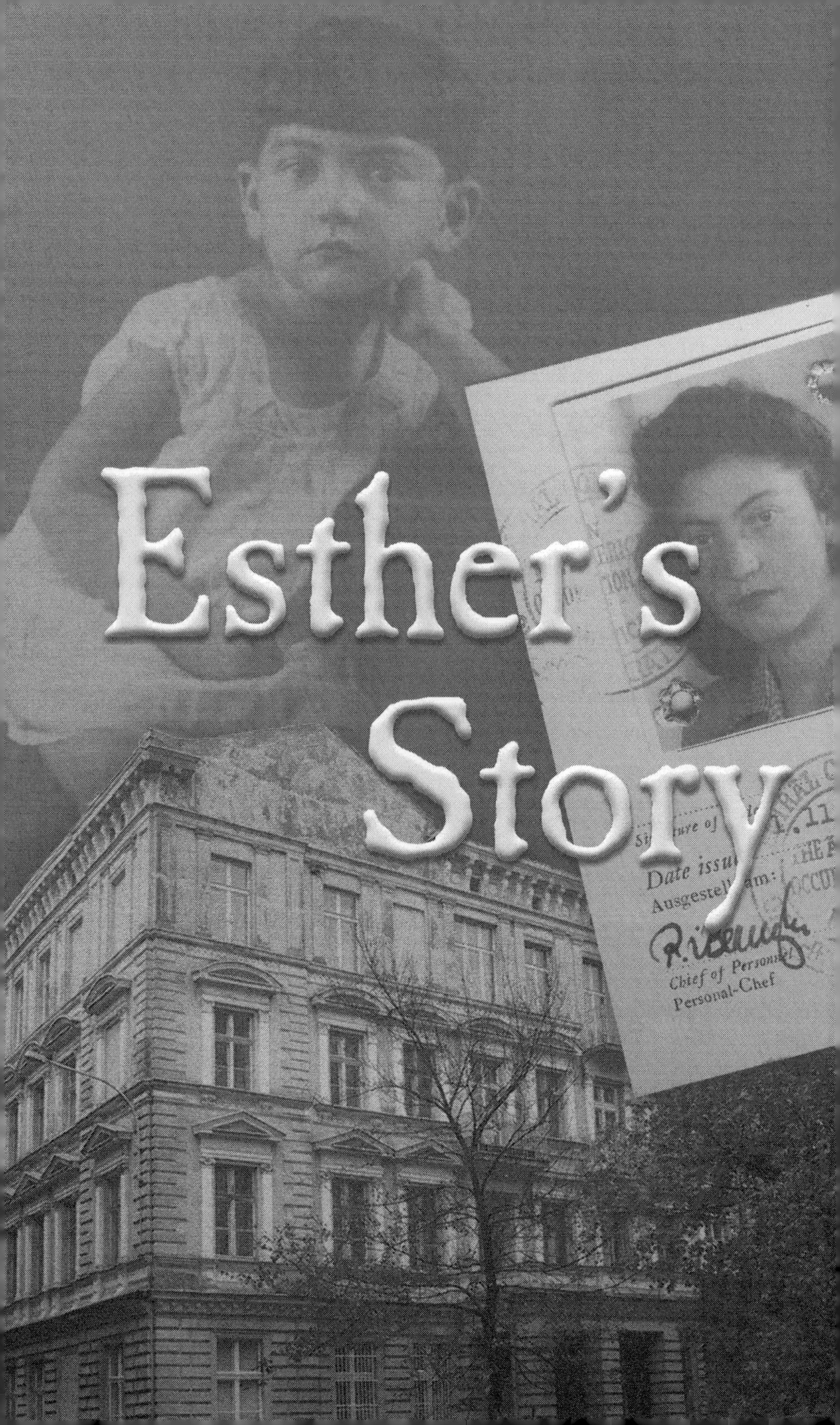
Esther's Story
Date issu
Ausgestell am:
Personal-Chef

# PREFACE

We lived in Lodz. It was Poland's second-largest city, with 600,000 inhabitants, half of whom were Jewish. There was a thriving Jewish community with private religious and secular schools, Jewish theater, Jewish newspapers in Yiddish and Polish, and Jewish hospitals. Even the Police Commissioner was Jewish, although he had converted to Catholicism. There was anti-Semitism, but it was not blatant because of the large Jewish population of the city and the presence of a strong Socialist party, which had less of an anti-Jewish bias. Lodz also had a population of ethnic Germans, who had their own schools and Protestant churches (rare in Catholic country like Poland was and still is). The Germans had come to Lodz sometime in the 19th century as specialists in the textile industry, which they founded and helped develop and run, and they would become important players in the drama that unfolded with Hitler's war.

# A HAPPY CHILDHOOD

My earliest memories of our apartment at 6 Rzgowska Street are not too clear. This apartment, a third floor walk-up, was the place where my sister, Halina, and I were born; where my parents, Israel and Rose Gutman, conceived their plans for the future; and it was the starting point for our little family's upward mobility. It consisted of one room and a kitchen, which also served as my mother's workshop, with a place for a cot for the maid. The maid was usually a farm girl who would come to the big city to get a small salary and enough food to forget the hunger she suffered back in her village. I remember this apartment as being very large and sunny, although maybe because I was such a small child the space around me seemed to be so generous. The focus of the main room was a large tile stove, which played a role in mother's strategies to get me to eat properly. I was a miserable eater, and my mother would bribe me by putting me on top of that stove, feeding me a spoonful of cereal, or whatever it was that I refused to eat, playing one record on the phonograph, and singing a song. For the next spoonful she had to think of something more exciting and stimulating to do.

I believe I had a happy childhood. Before my sister was born, I was the only girl in the extended family. While I was bright and cheerful, I was also temperamental and spoiled, and everybody would make a big fuss over me.

My mother had two brothers living in the neighborhood. One was Uncle Fishel, who was married to Aunt Dora, whom I adored. The other was Uncle Simon, who was married to Aunt Esther, whom I liked but not as much as Aunt Dora. Uncle Fishel had a fiery temperament, but Aunt Dora was a model of patience and goodness. If there was a problem or illness in the family, she was always there to lend a helping hand with love and care. As a matter of fact, when I woke up after my appendectomy in 1939, hers was the very first face I saw.

Once, when I was about three years old, I decided to take a walk or maybe I wanted to run away from home. I just picked myself up, sneaked out of the house, and wound up at my Aunt Dora's house. My mother was frantic with worry—running around the streets asking all passers-by if they'd seen a little girl in a white dress, but nobody could give her any information. There was no telephone at our apartment, nor at my aunt's house. Finally someone had the idea to go and check at my Uncle Fishel and Aunt Dora's house, and sure enough, I was there. I don't remember what the punishment was, but I am sure I was not rewarded for that deed. My mother frequently talked about my unruliness and disobedience.

I was already a big girl of four in the summer of 1928, when my sister was due to be born. I remember visiting my mother's older sister, Rivka, in a small town called Zarki when my mother was very heavy with the baby. We took many long walks in the forest and picked mushrooms, berries, and nuts. When I needed to pee, I refused to go into the bushes like everybody else. I insisted that I go on my potty. And, sure enough my family indulged me and carried a potty for me on all our excursions. (This story was told to me by one of my cousins, my Aunt Rivka's son, Shlomo Zelcer. Shlomo lost his wife and two little girls in the war, and afterward my father introduced him to his cousin, Cesia, who had lost her husband. After a short courtship Shlomo and Cesia got married and had two children, Rebeka and Chaskalae, known as Charlie. Shlomo died in 1992.)

We went back to our Rzgowska Street apartment when it was time for Halina to be born. (In those days, childbirth usually took place at home, and the notion of going to the hospital to have a baby was alien to most women. Just the thought of a hospital would evoke images of incurability and death. Giving birth was viewed as a natural function, not a disease, and took place at home with the help of a midwife.) I was shipped to Aunt Dora's house for the event, and after the baby was born I was brought back home to meet my new sister. What I saw was a strange being wriggling on my bed. I felt displaced and replaced. I felt strong resentment and jealousy that lasted for a very long time.

Within a year of Halina's birth my parents felt that we needed a better apartment, one in a neighborhood that would be advantageous for my mother's growing dressmaking/couture business. She hoped that in a better neighborhood she would be able to develop a higher class of clientele. Also, I believe, since there were two children to consider now, my parents felt that in a nicer neighborhood we would have a greater chance for betterment. I think that this attitude toward upward mobility in American society may have had roots in Europe; people everywhere have the same instincts for survival and the improvement of living conditions.

Another reason for moving was the fact that my mother's mother was going to live with us. My grandmother lived with us for about a year at our new house on Moniuszki Street, until she had a stroke at the age of 82. She died at home, just about a week after the stroke. I remember that she loved to hear me and Halina sing to her.

Our new home was uptown, in the very center of town. Moniuszki Street was small, consisting only of one city block, but it was very beautiful. It was lined with apartment houses, most of which had walled-in gardens. Children in this neighborhood did not play in the street or in the courtyard. Children played at home or were escorted to the park by their nannies or mothers. There was no unsupervised play of children anywhere, anytime.

Our new apartment was so much larger than our previous one, and much more convenient for my mother's business. My parents' bedroom also served as my mother's trying-on room. The dining room served as mother's waiting room. My sister slept in a small living room (we called it the "salonik") until I permitted her to move into my room with me. The maid's room was used as a workroom, and the maid had to make

do with a cot in the kitchen. There was a small room that was my grandmother's. My room was very large and rented separately from our neighbors, the landlords and owners of the building. It was incorporated into
the apartment at a later date. This beautifully furnished room had two
huge windows that opened inward. I spent many hours sitting there
watching trees come back to life in the spring, watching lilacs bloom,
listening to the birds sing, with the whole garden budding, chirping,
rustling, and filling me with anticipation, while I dreamed romantic
dreams of handsome boys, and great friendships with my best girlfriends.
In the winter everything was covered with fluffy white snow, which made
me feel so cozy in the warm house. The smell of snow made me hurry up,
get dressed, and get my skates.

For me, skating was synonymous with happiness. I dreamt of
being another Sonja Henje, with a great career as a figure skater, of being
able to soar and float on my skates with great ease and grace. I imagined
myself the center of attention and admiration of great crowds. I imagined
myself as being beautiful and being the very best skater around. My
dreams varied according to my moods and the prevalent trends in school.
At various times I wanted to be a radio announcer, a writer, an actress, an
archeologist, and a professional figure skater.

# DISTANT RUMBLINGS OF TROUBLE

During the World Olympic Games in Berlin in 1936 we were glued to the radio listening to the cruel proclamations of Adolph Hitler, who would not let the "American Negro" athlete, Jesse Owens, participate in the games, since he was of an "inferior" race. We were quite upset with these happenings, not realizing that this Hitler was the man who would decide our future fate. We also listened to the news on the radio. My parents were very interested in the political situation in Europe, particularly in Germany, and my father especially was very troubled by the news.

Around this time, my Uncle Shmuel from Radom, one of my father's younger brothers, decided to sell his house and factory and emigrate to Palestine with his wife who was pregnant with their second child. My father willingly lent him 15,000 Zlotys, enabling my uncle to travel to Palestine as a "capitalist," which was defined as someone in possession of 1,000 pounds sterling. Capitalists could emigrate to Palestine legally and establish residence there. It was a great deal of money at that time, but my uncle repaid the loan, investing the remaining money in a business venture in Tel Aviv. During the riots in 1937 the Arabs burned his business down to the ground, and my uncle in desperation wanted to return to Poland. My father wrote to him, urging him to stay there. If life became unbearable for them, he would send them the money for the return trip with his family, but in the meantime he asked him to remain in Palestine because life in Poland was becoming more and more unpleasant for Jews.

My father also wanted to emigrate to Palestine, and we could have easily put together enough money to emigrate as capitalists. But my mother was against it. She found life in Poland good enough and from what she heard, life in Palestine was quite difficult with a new language, harsh climate, and no household help.

The decision was made that we would not emigrate as yet. My father talked about taking a trip to Palestine to buy some property and invest some money there while waiting in Poland to see what happened. In the meantime life went on as usual. My mother's couture business was developing very nicely. Her income grew, and managing the money my mother was making kept my father busy. As time progressed and the rumblings of the coming war were getting closer, my father decided to invest in real estate and in articles that would be in short supply during wartime, including leather, cotton, and rice. He remembered times during World War I, when these things were almost unavailable. He and his cousin, who was also named Israel Gutman, became partners in various business ventures. Since Jews were not granted import or export licenses, they acquired a Gentile third partner who could front the business. They were granted licenses to import cotton and rice from Egypt and to export sugar to England. They also invested in a modern apartment building in a fine new neighborhood. This gave them a sense of financial security.

Our daily routine rarely changed. We had school six days a week, with Saturdays off, since ours was a Jewish school. I was doing very well in school. Learning came very easily to me, though I was by nature lazy and careless. If I paid attention in class, all I required in order to retain the information was to glance once or twice through the text, and I had it. I participated in class discussions, and if I did not have the lesson pat, I managed to fudge, since I was very articulate. Thanks to my voluminous reading I acquired a tremendous vocabulary. This helped me to hold the attention of my teachers and the classmates and build a reputation as a very good speaker. I also participated in all school plays and was a very good actress (on a high school level). We would put on plays and dance performances like any high school, be it in Poland, or the United States.

Youngsters have the same desires and dreams and ways of expressing them no matter where they live, and no matter what conditions. Life experience has taught me that people's needs differ very little regardless of where they live. Once their basic needs are satisfied—food and shelter—other needs arise. Better shelter, better food, better clothes, better schools, vacation savings, and financial security for their old age and for their children's and grandchildren's future.

My parents built their lives on these foundations without realizing that there was a monster, lurking in our future, which would destroy everything in spite of the most carefully laid plans.

When I look back at my childhood I believe it was a happy one. It was not the custom then to delve that much into feelings and introspection. We took what came at face value. If you had a problem you solved it. If you couldn't solve it you lived with it and made the best you could of the situation. There were no psychologists and no psychotherapy, single or group. You went to a psychiatrist only if you were "crazy." The very word psychiatrist was synonymous with mental disease and shame, something not mentioned in public. So, if people had problems—marital or otherwise—they either solved them themselves or lived with these problems and hid them from their neighbors.

I have fond memories of my father. He would come to pick us up from school on Sundays, and sometimes he would take us for a ride in Poniatowski Park in a horse-drawn cab, which we loved. Then he would tell us all kinds of stories from the war, when he was drafted into the Polish army to fight the Bolsheviks in 1920. According to his stories, he went as far as Kiev, where he contracted typhus and wound up in a field hospital, while the whole Polish army had to retreat all the way back to Warsaw. He would also answer all kinds of questions regarding the workings of the world. I thought at that time that my father was the smartest man in the world.

Our mother never had time for us. An excellent dressmaker and designer, she employed about 20 girls in her business. She had a great reputation for exquisite taste and fine craftsmanship. She worked hard and made a lot of money. The feeling of financial independence gave her great pride. Also, thanks to her high earnings we could afford to be sent to a private school, to have winter vacations in the mountains and summers in the country, to live in the best neighborhood, and to have all the little amenities that we would not have been able to afford on my father's salary alone, although it was decent. On rare occasions, when my mother made time to sit down and talk was with us, it was when we were sick. Then she would let her imagination run wild, telling us all kinds of fairy tales. She read a lot and could make up stories to capture a child's imagination.

Our family was not a religious one. My parents would go to the synagogue on High Holy days and for Yizkor services on Passover and Yom Kippur. We kept a kosher home but did not observe the Sabbath. My father worked on Saturdays till 1 p.m. My mother did not work on Saturdays, but she kept her shop open on Sundays. We had no school on Saturdays, but attended school on Sundays.

The question of religion never came up in our home. Religion went as far as instruction in school (it was a part of the school curriculum), but  application was left to the home. We knew that we were Jewish, that we observed Jewish holidays and had them off from school, that Kashrut was observed in the house as a matter of fact, but I don't know the exact extent of its thoroughness. The importance of observing religious rituals was never discussed.

All during my grandmother's life my mother was very scrupulous about lighting Sabbath candles. After her mother's death there were times when my mother skipped that ritual. It didn't bother me one way or another. We knew about Palestine and had loose information about the Zionist movement. My mother was a member of WIZO (World Women's Zionist organization), and my sister attended a WIZO nursery school. I also knew that some of my friends had a loose association with some Zionist organization—like Hashomer Hatzair—but my knowledge was very vague. At school we were not allowed to join any organizations except those approved by the school authorities, like the Red Cross or

Winter Help for the Underprivileged.

We children were not instructed by our parents in the development of a social conscience. We knew that there were poor people, since we saw them in the street, and beggars would come to the door to ask for handouts. We gave them pennies or food. Also, my mother was very helpful in supporting her family members, who were less fortunate than we were. She was constantly sending money to her sisters in Jedrzejow, bringing their children to Lodz, helping them to establish themselves in the big city, helping them in finding apartments, furnishing them, and then helping them in establishing means of support. Before any holidays, there were trips to the home of her oldest brother, who lived in our old neighborhood, to bring him baskets of food and the best of everything. My mother was fortunate not to lack in anything, but she never forgot that there were those in her own family who had less and that she had an obligation to help. And that was the atmosphere of compassion that I grew up with. There was no public recognition, no publicity, no commemorative dinners, no rewards for good deeds. These deeds were done because they had to be done; and no fuss was made about it.

There was compulsory elementary school in the Poland of 1918–1939. This education was available at no cost, and all children— Poles, Jews, ethnic Germans, Ukrainians, and Gypsies—had to attend school. School began with first grade at age seven and finished at 14 with the seventh grade. From there, children could go on to high school ("Gimnazjum"), to trade school, or to work. There were state maintained high schools with minimal tuition costs, from which Jewish students were practically excluded. Gentile children from poorer families could obtain scholarships to these institutions and not entirely on merit. Even the brightest Jewish children would rarely receive a scholarship like that, especially in rural areas or small towns. There were private high schools with very high tuitions. These were either Jewish or Christian, and the student population in these schools was mixed. There were Jewish students in non-Jewish schools, but never any Christian students in Jewish schools.

My sister and I attended a private, secular Jewish school from the first grade on. In a private school a child could begin the first grade at the age of six and didn't have to attend the 7th grade. After graduating from the 6th grade we took an entrance examination, which when passed entitled us to enter the 1st class of the Gimnazjum. After four years of general programs in the humanities, including languages, history, social studies, math, sciences, etc., there was another examination to enter the "Liceum." This entailed two years of more specialized study in either humanities or sciences. After completion of that program there was another difficult comprehensive matriculation examination. Success on that exam entitled a student to enter the university in any desired discipline. The education obtained throughout the 12 years would be an equivalent of an American education in depth and quality. A certificate of matriculation from the Gimnazjum and Liceum carried great prestige, social and economic. It guaranteed better job opportunities and social standing.

## THE SUMMER OF '39

The summer of 1939 was beautiful. I had just celebrated my 15th birthday and thought myself very grown up. I considered Halina, who was only 11, still a baby. We always rented a small cottage for the summer, and that summer our parents sent my sister and me to the country about 15 km out of the city with our maid. Since I just had an appendectomy, my father's boss was kind enough to have his chauffeur drive us there. The feeling of luxury and privilege was marvelous. We didn't own a car. We were quite comfortably well off, but very few people in our circumstances owned automobiles in Poland at that time. My stay at a small private clinic had been very pleasant. I felt pampered as a princess. I was the center of attention, I had my family's concern, and lots and lots of friends came to visit. I felt I could do no wrong.

For the first time in my life I felt important, attractive, and popular. My being popular in school and after school began the previous winter with my figure skating. I was very good and I spent a lot of time at the skating rink, even at the expense of doing homework. I looked attractive and graceful, and many boys wanted to be introduced to me. (In those days in our circles a boy didn't just walk up to a girl and start a conversation. One had to be introduced.) My "boyfriend" Samuel (Samek) Herszkowicz visited me a few times during that ten-day stay at the hospital; he brought me a book by P. G. Wodehouse. It was very funny,

12

but I couldn't laugh because of the pain at the incision site. My "love affair" with Samek was so innocent. I met Samek through his cousin, my friend Halina Kupfer. He would be at her home when I visited her on Saturday mornings. He was a tall, scrawny teenager with bad skin and awkward motions. He impressed me so much because he was a math whiz and he played the piano well. I was very impressed with his performance of Liszt's Hungarian Rhapsody. He had very long fingers and large hands. To me he was the personification of a genius. I was so bedazzled by him that I would walk a couple of extra blocks on the way to school in the morning, just to see him take off his school cap in greeting. I never saw him after the war.

We had a wonderful time that summer in the country. Although the clouds of war were gathering, and the thunder of future disasters was heard in the distance, we tried to ignore the foreboding. My friends and I would meet, discuss books like the new Gone With the Wind, try to speak English with one another, and make believe we were foreigners in Poland. This was just a game we played for no particular reason. We would go for walks, go swimming, and tell each other secrets. We would fall in and out of love for a week or so, and never mention it to the boys in question. Looking back at these times, I realize we were desperately clinging to our childhood innocence.

One boy's father had just returned from the World Zionist Congress Conference in Geneva. He brought very grim news; war was approaching. Hitler would probably start it, and the Jews had nowhere to go. Nobody wanted them. The future for the Jews in Europe, especially in Poland looked bleak. The boy's father was making arrangements to flee from Poland with his family.

My parents visited us on weekends with the exception of the first two weeks in July, which my mother spent in a spa, as she usually did. During that time my father would commute nightly to the country from the city. In the middle of July my mother left the spa to spend the rest of the summer with us. Around that same time, Hitler's belligerent actions and boasting were coming on stronger. He was demanding the corridor of Danzig, a free city since the Treaty of Versailles in 1918 and Poland's only access to the Baltic Sea. It was impossible for the Polish Government to comply with this demand. War loomed inevitable. A general mobilization was called on August 27th. Mother decided it was time to return to the city. Father was of draft age but had not been called up yet.

We got home on Tuesday, August 29, 1939. The streets were plastered with placards of the mobilization. Men were standing several deep, reading excitedly about their units being called up. We expected Dad to be mobilized imminently. There was a frantic activity in the air. We were caught up in the amazing feeling of excitement. Everywhere a spirit of preparedness and high patriotism prevailed. No sacrifice would be too high for our country. We would destroy the German swine! He had no chance with us! Adding to that elevated mood, the weather was unusually beautiful. The sky was cloudless, the air warm and fragrant.

# THE GERMAN INVASION

On Friday morning, September 1, 1939, we woke up to the news on the radio that the Germans had invaded Poland without declaring war. Our hearts froze. What would happen now? People remembered that during World War I German soldiers and officers were courteous and polite. Compared to Czarist Russian soldiers they were gentlemen. The Germans did take our men for forced labor to dig trenches, but they were always well behaved. They never touched women and children. Would they be different now? Considering the possibilities, people decided that it would be wise if the men left for a while until the situation cleared. Still, there were feelings of fear and uncertainty about the Germans' actions, now that their system was so different from the old one of a quarter of a century ago.

And so, men of all ages—Jews and non-Jews alike—ran. Most of them ran to Warsaw, which was declared an open city. Surely, the Germans would honor that declaration. Of course the capital would be safe. These were the sentiments of the people who fled. Later, we found out that it was a deliberate plan of the Germans to incite the population to flee their homes in order to cause chaos and demoralization. There were rumors that the Polish Army was retreating. There were also rumors that the Polish Army was victorious. The Polish government was issuing instructions trying to prepare us for a gas war. People who did not own gas masks were instructed to use gauze soaked in bicarbonate of soda. All windowpanes were to be crisscrossed with tape, and a black-out was in effect. All windows had to be covered tightly at night so that there were no lights visible on the outside. The air raids and sounds of bombs falling began from the second day of the war.

On the third day I was on an errand to the stationery store when I heard an air raid siren go off. There were explosions nearby. After a few minutes an "All Clear," was sounded. I heard people say that an apartment house on Bandurskiego Street was hit and a number of people were killed. I knew that my parents owned an apartment house at that address. I quickly went home to find that the story was true. The property was hit and eight people perished. It was the only apartment house in the whole city hit by a bomb ever. The Germans had aimed at a nearby military hospital and missed.

The Germans' modus operandi soon became apparent. From now on the city was bombed intermittently, although the bombings were not too effective. We spent most of our nights in the bomb shelter in the cellar of our apartment building. We had lived in our apartment for over ten years but never knew any of our neighbors until we slept in the shelters with them.

The rumors continued to spread wildly. The Germans were approaching. The Polish Army was routed. The Polish Army was advancing. One thing seemed to be clear: In order to preserve our fighting force, all able-bodied men should leave and go east. They should escape the Germans and go toward the unoccupied Polish territories east of the river Bug. Roads were clogged with refugees. German planes relentlessly strafed them. Many civilians were killed.

Meanwhile, the Russians, in accordance with their pact with the Germans, were reportedly approaching the Polish border, westward, towards the river Bug. If this were true, then there would be nothing to worry about. The Russians for sure would not hurt the civilian population. According to reports coming from that direction there was some regard for human life and safety. The general wisdom was that the men should leave temporarily and return when things settled down. Then the families would be together again for the duration of the war. We all had these delusions, Jews as well as Gentiles.

My father, his boss, Mr. Goldblum, and two other men got into his boss's car, filled it with gasoline (which was at a premium and practically unavailable), gathered a sizable amount of money, and left for a while. My mother, sister, the maid, and I were left alone in the apartment. For company and protection (we thought we needed a man in the house) my father's cousin, Israel Gutman, along with his wife and two sons, moved in with us. They were afraid to remain in their neighborhood, with its working class, anti-Semitic population. We lived in the center of the city, which was considered to be an elegant upper-middle-class neighborhood.

On the first night after their arrival in the city, the Germans went to apartments, including ours, and very politely requested blankets, pillows, and bed linen for the officers to be billeted with families in the building. We were frightened, and gave them the items they asked for. We were amazed at their politeness. Were these people really villains? They seemed quite nice. The next morning they returned the borrowed articles with profuse thanks. In the streets they were polite, saluting older people. We were stunned. It could not be true. And, it was not. These were the first army troops, simple conscripts not yet poisoned by the Nazi doctrine.

Two days later, other troops came in. These Germans were different. They took old Jews to clean the streets and beat them. They looted "requisitioned" Jewish stores. Requisitioning was issuing receipts for the merchandise they took. The issued receipts were worthless, since there was nobody to appeal to for payment. Still, these were sporadic events, and they did not seem to be organized. I believe this behavior was encouraged by the German authorities, but without a specific plan.

In the meantime, Warsaw was under siege, even though it was declared an open city. We listened to the radio anxiously, hearing reports of terrible bombings, destruction, lack of food and water. The Red Cross continuously read lists of refugees from other cities, and once I heard my father's name. Now we knew that he was in Warsaw, but Warsaw was crumbling and burning. Would he come home to us? If so when and how? How was he going to look and feel?

We were very unhappy at home. My mother did not get along with my father's cousin's wife. We had no privacy, and there was tension and bitterness fueled by constant bickering. There were food shortages. We had to get up at four in morning to stand in line to buy a loaf of bread and a quart of milk. Since I was young and a girl—boys would not be sent out for fear of their being beaten by the Germans or the Poles—I was elected to go with our maid, Bronia, so we could get two loaves. She was still living with us and helping with housework. Many times when I was almost at the head of the line, I was picked out by the Polish police and sent to the end. They said I did not need the bread since I was Jewish.

The Germans tried to normalize the everyday lives of the citizens. Schools, even Jewish schools, were ordered open. So we started attending school in the academic year 1939–1940. When the Nazis entered our town, the streets were full of people wearing swastika armbands and flying swastika banners. These were people with German names, descendants of Germans, who had settled in Poland many generations ago. Now they came out to cheer their new leader, their "savior," who arrived to personally greet his people. They called themselves "Volksdeutsche," ethnic Germans. This was a very large percentage of the population of Lodz. Hordes of Volksdeutsche eagerly embraced their "liberators" and the freedom to do as they pleased. They tormented people regardless of age—old people, young people, even school children. Soon, every day during morning attendance at school it was obvious that many students and faculty were missing. Some would come in late with bandages on their heads and bruises on their faces, their clothes torn and grimy. The scene became familiar: Jews caught and forced to work by the Volksdeutsche for their amusement. The work was mostly unnecessary and designed to humiliate, like picking up horse droppings with bare hands, scrubbing sidewalks, and carrying heavy objects, especially if the victim was old.

I can't forget the morning when our physics teacher, Dr. Gutman, walked into class late. He was a man in his fifties, short and rotund. We had nicknamed him "Moonface" because of his round florid face. That morning his face was cut up and he had a heavy bandage on his head. His eyes were wild, focusing on nothing, his speech was impaired, his clothes were in shreds, and he was limping. He could not conduct class that morning. The next day we heard he committed suicide. He just couldn't live with the humiliation.

We attended school from about the 20th of September till the beginning of December when our family left town. But I learned much. The poetry and literature we read at that time had a special flavor. Descriptions of beauty and goodness had an additional depth. Feelings were sharper. Colors were brighter. There was so much awareness of life. Maybe we sensed that those little moments of freedom would soon enough be taken away from us. All of us in school shared these feelings. It was amazing that classes were conducted in the most conventional way. There were quizzes, tests, homework assignments, etc. Most of the girls were from well-to-do homes, spoiled and accustomed to an easy life. We grew up without any responsibilities. But suddenly we wanted to learn and to discover new avenues.

I remember how it was with me. Before the war, I was a good student, bright and intelligent, but lazy. Learning came easily to me, but I never applied myself. I preferred skating, going to the movies, or reading novels rather than studying algebra or Latin. Now learning became a fun game. We challenged ourselves to retain as much information as possible, to absorb everything within our reach. It was as if we had a premonition that something would happen and all would be taken away from us and destroyed. There was a feverish desire to absorb and devour every little bit of knowledge. During that time I realized that one phase of my life had ended and another had begun. I stopped being an overindulgent, pampered child and joined the adult world. I stopped being a flighty, thoughtless teenager, with her head in the clouds, daydreaming and spinning fairy tales in the privacy of her mind. The time arrived when I had to take on some responsibilities of adulthood. The change in the political and economic situation around us reminded us that we couldn't remain children forever. Responsibilities of everyday life, like finding food, had to be delegated to us children. Suddenly our parents started treating us as adults. I even got along with Halina. We started talking, sharing reflections and comments on the adult world.

We continued to devour every bit of news from the radio. Radio Warsaw, heralded by the beloved Revolutionary Etude by Chopin, was still broadcasting lists of names of people stranded in the capital. While we had the comfort of knowing that our father was alive, the battle for Warsaw raged on. The Germans did not honor the International Conventions of Warsaw being declared an open city. They bombed it, they burned it, they left it in a smoking shambles. We all reacted to this news with the same impotent rage.

Warsaw finally surrendered after 28 days of desperate and hopeless fighting. The Germans entered the city and allowed the refugees to go home. My father returned. He was ragged, dirty, tired, and emaciated, but he was happy to be back. He was full of stories about the devastated capital, about the hunger, thirst, and death. This was the first time in the history of mankind, to our knowledge, that an invading army had waged a war against a civilian population. The Germans waged war by fire, hunger, fear, and intimidation. And they were winning this kind of a war. We were still not accustomed to this kind of treatment by the authorities.

# Flight From Lodz

After my father's return we tried to restore some normalcy into our lives. Dad tried to put his assets in order and assess his losses. First he raised money to repair the bombed apartment building so that the residents could move back. People needed living quarters, and we needed to protect our property. The railroad siding (the stretch of tracks where freight trains were stationed awaiting distribution and shipments of merchandise) where our sugar, rice, and raw cotton were stored had been completely plundered, but a leather warehouse that Dad owned in partnership with his cousin had not as yet been touched. That was something. The partners were unable to sell that merchandise and obtain some liquid funds. Nobody wanted to part with cash in U.S. dollars or gold in these uncertain times. At any rate, it did not matter, because a few days later the Germans emptied the warehouse into lorries. They even gave my father a receipt for that load. That was the end of the Gutman fortune.

We were left only with what we could carry in addition to a sizable amount of Zlotys in cash, and some U.S. dollars that my parents kept in the house. It would have to suffice. On November 11, the Polish national Day of Independence, the Germans dynamited the monument of the Polish hero Tadeusz Kosciuszko in midtown Lodz. They announced that Jews had destroyed the monument. In "revenge" the Poles burned down the most beautiful synagogue on Kosciuszki Avenue. From that time on events were happening with lightning speed. Our dad was caught for forced labor by a man he had considered to be his friend before the war. I don't remember his name. He was a Volksdeutsche who had to show how deeply he was imbued with the new Nazi doctrine. This "friend" caught my father in the street and took him to do a lot of demeaning work, like picking up horse droppings and washing the streets with his bare hands, and carrying heavy loads. All the while he was beaten, cursed, and humiliated.

My father returned home completely broken. He wanted to leave the big city for some smaller place. His brother Abraham, a well-to-do man, lived with his family in his own house in Chmielnik, his hometown, and the town where my father was born. After hearing from my father, my uncle was eager to have us join him and his family. An argument arose between my parents. My mother flatly refused to move. She said that she had not left the narrow-minded mentality of a small town years ago only to have to bring her daughters to live in one now. It was amazing. Either my mother was genuinely ignorant or she refused to acknowledge the tragedy of our situation and the fact that we had no options.

My father argued that this was to be only a temporary arrangement, that the war was not going to last too long, and that we would be able to return soon enough. He reminded her that during World War I Uncle Fishel and his family had fled the Germans and went to Pinsk in the eastern part of the country, survived the war there, and returned home afterward. Their apartment remained untouched. He tried to persuade her that now, since England and France had joined the war, the Germans could never win. Anyway, he said, we would not be able to stay in our apartment on Moniuszki Street too long since the Germans had established a Gestapo post in the police station across the street. And since this was a very fine neighborhood, he argued the Germans would not allow Jews to remain there.

That was the mood in which Dad left for Chmielnik. Again the four females were left home. We tried to live as if everything were normal. Halina and I attended school and shopped for food. We made do with what staples were in the house. All this "normalcy" felt tenuous.

In the meantime, there were new laws being proclaimed by the German authorities every day. People had to turn in their radio receivers under penalty of death. All savings accounts were frozen indefinitely, and only small sums could be withdrawn at a time. These ordinances applied to everyone, not just Jews.

Soon rumors spread that Jews would no longer be permitted to live anywhere except for the Baluty district. Baluty, in the northern part of the city, was inhabited by very poor workers and craftspeople, mainly Jewish. It was actually a slum, with dilapidated buildings and no sewer system.

In the meantime, we awaited news from our father in Chmielnik. In the middle of December, a messenger arrived at our home with a note from Dad. It said that a horse-drawn lorry would be waiting for us at the railroad junction in Skierniewice to take us to Chmielnik. Mother was practically hysterical. She flatly refused to go to Chmielnik. We, the two young children, had to argue with her that this would only be a temporary measure, that we would leave home for the duration of the war, that the war would not last too long. We, the children, had to persuade an adult and try to reverse her decision. I once again realized that my childhood was over and that realization sustained me in the argument. Finally, Mama gave up. We would leave immediately. We packed, but we left our summer clothes, because we convinced ourselves that by then the war would certainly be over.

We took our Aunt Chana (my father's and Abraham's sister) and her husband and four children with us, and of course Bronia. It was an arduous journey. The winter was harsh. There was a lot of snow and a bitter frost. It seemed like the whole world was frozen. We began our flight to a tenuous haven on December 16, 1939.

## LIFE IN KIELCE

After a tiring trip we arrived in Kielce, a medium-sized city with a population of about 50,000. Kielce was a compromise for my mother. She had cousins there. She refused to go all the way to Chmielnik, refused to capitulate to a simple little thing like Hitler's war. We were well received by her cousins, the Burstyns, and that was where out father met us. We had missed him terribly, and he had missed us. The reunion was emotional, and for a while we hoped that we would be able to wait out the war in a relatively peaceful way. We wanted to believe that the war would soon be over and all would be right with the world.

We spent 15 months in Kielce in the apartment of an elderly widow, a lovely and kind woman named Mrs. Graus. All citizens had to register the size of their apartments with the Jewish Community Council, which would assign living quarters to refugees accordingly. There were many refugees. People were constantly leaving their own homes in hopes of finding a safe haven somewhere else. There were quite a number of people from Lodz, which the Germans in the meantime annexed to the Third Reich and renamed Litzmannstadt. They started introducing the Nuremberg Laws there, and began the creation of a separate Jewish ghetto.

Mrs. Graus's apartment consisted of two rooms, a kitchen, and a corridor. There was running cold water in the kitchen, and tile stoves supplied the heat. There was no bathroom, and the toilet (actually an outhouse) was in the courtyard. We did not mind it. It was ours, and we were a family, and Bronia was still with us. We had to say good-bye to her in April of 1940, since according to the new regulations Jews were not allowed to employ or even live under the same roof as Aryans. So, Bronia packed her things and tearfully departed to her home village near Lodz.

Of course, before leaving Lodz we had sent to Bronia's parents some valuables from our apartment for safekeeping, like rugs, crystals, china, and more valuable household articles. I didn't even know her parents' names, or the name of the village. The most important factor was trust, and we were sure that by the summer we would be back home. By that time the people we trusted would return our belongings to us. In retrospect it seems so ridiculous, that all throughout these times, when we saw that the world was actually burning and falling apart around our heads, we still had this stubborn capacity for self-delusion.

About that same time, the Germans shipped a few thousand Austrian Jews to Kielce. Most of them came from Vienna. These were people whose parents came to Austria many years ago from Poland and had neglected to obtain Austrian citizenship. They lived in that culture, and a whole new generation of Jewish people grew up as Austrians. All of a sudden they were told that they were not Austrian, but Polish (OstJuden) Jews. They were told to pack 20 kg and get out. Of course, they received free transportation to Kielce. The Jewish Community Council had the responsibility of allocating these people among the existing apartments, regardless of how many people already occupied them. So, two of these Austrian Jews were allocated to Mrs. Graus's apartment, and one day two lovely ladies arrived with suitcases in their hands.

They were middle-aged (maybe 37 to 39 years old). They were forced to leave their families back in Vienna. One of them was fortunate that her mother and children were able to leave Germany on the last ship to the United States. They were delightful women, one of them an opera singer. We got along beautifully and spent many hours talking, reminiscing, and singing. They introduced me to opera music and also to the Yiddish song "Raizale," which I loved and eagerly learned to sing.

So, to all appearances, life was running smoothly in Kielce in

Mrs. Graus's apartment. We had food, we had one another, we had nice friends and pleasant evenings after curfew. It seemed feasible to think that the war would be soon over, all of us would return to our homes, and everything would be as before.

In the meantime, the news from the front lines was not good. The Germans conquered France, Belgium, Holland, Denmark, and Norway, and were making preparations for the conquest of Great Britain. Jews were being taken to labor camps. Large amounts of money were being collected by the Jewish Community Council to bribe the German officials to ease the anti-Jewish decrees. We still had some money, so we could buy food on the black market, which was semi-official.

One day my father was taken to a labor camp about 15 km from town. We were stunned. This couldn't happen to us. Something had to be done. In the meantime rumors started circulating that the Germans intended to create a ghetto in Kielce and resettle all the Jews living in other districts of town. Mother, Halina, and I felt helpless. A decision had to be made. Since our father kept in touch with his brother in Chmielnik, we knew that there would be room for us with them. The only problem was how to get Dad out of that accursed camp? We decided that I would go to that place (called Wisniowka) and try to bribe the commandant of the camp. It seemed quite easy. It was still within the law to travel short distances, so actually it was not such a big deal. So on a nice spring day I got into a horse-drawn cab and went to that camp. I went to the camp office, which was run by a Pole who called himself a Volksdeutsche. (The privileges of making such a declaration were countless.) I spoke to him and really cannot recall what I told him. I still don't know what happened, whether he was taken in by my innocence and sincerity or perhaps moved by whatever was left of his conscience. At any rate, he released my father after a sizable "donation" was made to the "Red Cross." We were happy, my father and I, as we set out on the way home, to Mrs. Graus's apartment on foot. We didn't even feel the 15 km stroll as tiring. We were received at the apartment with kisses and tears of joy. The next day we packed and left for Chmielnik, never to return to our peaceful apartment with the sweet ladies in it.

## CHMIELNIK

We arrived at my father's brother's house in Chmielnik in April of 1941. Uncle Abraham was a handsome redhead of about 38 years of age. He was widowed at a young age and left with two young daughters. He soon remarried and lived with his wife, Esther, her mother, his two daughters, and a delightful little son named Moshele, who at that time was about three years old. They occupied a rambling old house of four rooms, a small kitchen, and a large garden. There was no running water in the house, heat was supplied by tile stoves in the rooms, like in Kielce, and there was a spotless outhouse in the garden. The outhouse was not too bad in spring or summer. But on a winter evening, with the temperature below freezing, to sit there with a bare bottom was not one of life's greatest pleasures. But one gets used to everything and this would not be the worst thing we would have to get used to. Our uncle and his family received us warmly and gave us the use of a bedroom for our parents, and the kitchen for Halina and me to sleep in. We got along fine. We did not complain and tried to arrange our life as best we could.

In Chmielnik, my mother's talent and expertise as a dressmaker and designer came to good use again. Some Polish ladies from the surrounding area found out about Mother's reputation, and started flocking to her with requests to update their wardrobes. Mother took on these tasks and was paid handsomely not with money, which was by then almost worthless, but with produce. We had plenty of eggs, butter, flour, sugar, and everything edible except for meat. The quality of the food we had helped us stay well. People who had to depend on the rations allotted to the Jews by the authorities were starving to death. If they didn't starve, diseases got them. The people, and especially children, were undernourished, underclothed, homeless, and abandoned. It may sound selfish to have people eat while others are starving, but no matter, how much one wanted to share one's food, there would never be enough to go around. Food was the key to survival, at least on a temporary basis. Once you had food, you thought you could make it to the end of the war, which would be over, maybe not too soon, but soon enough.

Chmielnik was a little town of 10,000 people, 8,000 of whom were Jews. Nevertheless, before the war the Jews did not have a representative to the Town Hall, nor did they have anyone employed by the government. There was no Jewish mailman, no Jewish policeman, Jewish attorney, or Jewish town official. There was no high school, no hospital. There were two doctors, one of them Jewish, and one feltcher (a sort of a barber-surgeon). But there was an elementary school to meet the demands of the compulsory education laws. If a Jewish family wanted their children to go to high school, they had to send them either to Kielce (30 km away), or to Busko-Zdroj (15 km away). The children would then have to pay boarding costs as well as tuition, and that was very expensive. At the time the war broke out there were only five Jewish children away at high school.

This was the cultural mecca to which we had come. As soon as we arrived in Chmielnik, I met a boy and a girl who were my second cousins. The girl, Lola, attended high school in Kielce, while her brilliant brother, Moniek, did not. He had more education and intelligence than any other youngster I had ever met before, even those with the best education available to them. Through these two I became friends with a whole lot of kids. We used to meet at someone's home to discuss and solve all the world's problems. We would assign books to read, and then discuss them. We would sing and dance (the only accompaniment was our humming). You just cannot take young people and tell them not to be young and live. As long as they are free to meet and interact, the life will burst from their souls.

There were some high school and university teachers who had been displaced from the big cities, who came to Chmielnik as refugees. They were looking for something to do and wanting to make a little money. These people formed groups of youngsters, with four or five to a group, and taught subjects in the high school curriculum of pre-war Poland. I belonged to such a group, as did my sister. Textbooks were available, and there was a great desire to study. These classes were conducted clandestinely; if we were caught, we would be punished, possibly shot. This great risk only made classes more appealing. As a safety measure, each meeting was held at a different house. We learned a lot without physics and chemistry laboratories, without physical education, and without many of the amenities of a private school education.

One day, as I walked with my father along the street, a lady called him over. This was Mrs. Minca Lederman, whom my father knew before he was married, and they hadn't seen each other in ages. She asked us inside the house to meet her husband and sons. We came in, and politely exchanged some pleasantries. There was Mr. Lederman, a very nice gentleman, and two boys, Szmulek or Sam, and Ezjel, known then as Salek. Sam was among the handful of Jewish students attending high school, while Salek was tutored privately at home and was taking passing examinations in Kielce as an "extern." We were introduced, and the two young gentlemen promptly turned their backs on me and continued with their interrupted conversation. Well, I didn't care for them either. Little did I know, I was meeting that day the people who would be extremely important in my life.

It turned out that Szmulek and Salek (Sam and Ezjel, as we now know them) were members of the same group of friends. And we saw more of them. Ezjel, though, held himself aloof. I liked him, maybe because he was different from anyone I'd ever met before. He was very handsome. He was tall, with a head of curly golden hair, which he held up high in the air. His eyes were the color of honey and had little lights in them. His skin was smooth without any pimple ever (I envied him that),

29

with a slight peachy fuzz on the cheeks. He always wore his shirt open at the neck, with the collar laid out of the jacket. He looked fearless and beautiful, at least in my eyes. I found his integrity, honesty, and simplicity appealing. There was nothing simplistic about him, and no artifice whatsoever. There was no naivete, though. Ideas were developed, thought and reasoned out. He had an uncompromising mind. There was only black and white, with no room for gray. A person in a particular situation was either good or bad. One's word was binding under any circumstances. These traits were so refreshing and made him so different from other boys. How could anyone with a bit of intelligence not find these qualities captivating, especially at a time of complete moral dissolution?

Of course it seemed to me that he was not even aware of my existence. That galled me. I liked him and was determined to make him notice me. I just needed a way to make myself attractive to him. I knew that looking pretty was not going to be enough. At any rate, he did not find me pretty. I was overweight, and I came from Lodz, the big city full of spoiled brats. The girls from my hometown did not have the best reputation. In those days a girl's reputation was still very important.

There was a girl in our group from my hometown by the name of Halina (a very popular name in those days). She was very bright, quiet, and shy. She liked Ezjel (I think quite a lot). One day, I went to the building where Ezjel was working at his job in the Sanitary Department. I brought with me a letter I'd written. Halina was there, too. We both waited for him to finish his work, and then we left the building together. Then I graciously asked Halina to give Ezjel and me a few moments alone together. She complied and left us. I gave Ezjel the note, which he read with bewilderment.

I always found it difficult to speak about my feelings. It was easier for me to express myself in writing. And so it was that time. I don't recall exactly what I wrote about, or how I worded my letter. I only remember that I suggested that we try to see each other more often and alone, that I liked him a lot, and that, given time, he might grow to like me. No matter how modest and perfect he was, Ezjel could not resist such flattery, and from then on we saw each other every free moment. Of course, in the back of my mind I felt a little guilty about how I had treated Halina, but with time that feeling faded, and we were still good friends.

During that time I was employed by the Jewish Council in the department of craft shops and artisan shops. It was a simple clerical job. My job consisted of keeping records of all kinds of sewing machines, cobblers' shops, etc. The Community Council could issue work permits, which gave people a false sense of security that they were productively occupied for the good of the German Reich, and thus could be exempt from forced labor. This was still quite innocent, and comparatively harmless, as far as safety of the Jewish community was concerned. I also did some volunteer work. On the same street as we lived there was a little Cheder, a religious school for little boys. The school was housed in a semi-basement room with a dirt floor that also served as a kitchen, living room, dining room, and bedroom for the teacher (the Melamed) and his family. In this room every morning, some scraps of the Torah knowledge were dispensed to a jostling, jumping, whining, and yelling group of about 20 snotty, sickly little boys of about five to eight years of age. I decided that these children should not be deprived of the treasure of a secular education, and I naturally determined that I should be the one who would dispense that knowledge. I don't exactly remember how long I lasted in my capacity as a distributor of all elementary education. In fact I tried to penetrate the thick prejudiced opinions of little boys, and they sure could be obstinate in their rejection of me. I came from a different world, and they hardly even understood my Polish. I was heartbroken and deeply disappointed at my inability to give some of my knowledge to these children.

My days were filled with my job and a growing preoccupation with the time spent with Ezjel. We would take long walks and talk, even though there really was no place to go for a walk. The little town of Chmielnik had an area designated as a Jewish ghetto, which fortunately was not fenced-in or walled-in from the outside community. A sign to the effect that this was a Jewish district and a "Seuchengebiet" or area of infectious diseases, and that entrance was forbidden to Aryans under severe punishment, was sufficient to keep non-Jews away. After a time this "severe punishment" was changed to "penalty of death." Of course, the same sign would proclaim that any Jew found outside of that area was liable to be punished by death. By that time, the words "death penalty" did not mean anything special in the Jewish community. Under the penalty of death were such transgressions as owning or operating a radio receiver, owning a little piece of fur, or possessing foreign currency, arms, or non-rationed food, and having any kind of relation with a non-Jew, traveling outside the ghetto, and using public transportation. The concept of punishment by death had somehow lost part of its threat because one becomes desensitized to constant danger. The Germans were very clever this way. The rules were gradual in their severity. One could adjust to tightened living conditions because they were incrementally imposed. It was like stretching exercises. If you do them regularly, a little more each day, after a while your muscles and joints are nice and stretched, and you don't even feel you are exercising. This was how it was with the German rules, regulations, and laws. Step two was only a little bit stronger than step one, and so on. Before we knew it, we were already at step ten, and hurting. But by then it was too late even to think of protesting.

And to whom could one protest? To the Germans? To the Jewish Community? To Poles? To parents? You could talk to your friends. And that was what we did.

# A YOUNG COUPLE IN LOVE

Ezjel and I walked and talked for hours. Since there was no park or pretty country lane to walk on and feel romantic, we could take long walks to the cemetery. There was an old Jewish cemetery, situated on a hill overlooking the town, and from there one could see the surrounding countryside. There were peaceful villages cuddled into furry forests. Small cottages with thatched roofs and tall chimneys that exhaled gentle wisps of smoke belied the reality of hunger, poverty, sickness, and hopelessness. The sun looked down equally bright on us and the somnolent villages. We looked around us, inhaling the pure air, listening to the stillness, and for a moment forgot where we were and what lay ahead of us. We were just two young people in love (or so we thought, because we didn't know any better), suspended in time. We sat close to one another, holding on tight, spinning tales of a future we knew we didn't have. We would start from a startling concept of a will to live and a right to do so, and come to a not less startling conclusion that we had absolutely no say in the course of our lives, that we were like lifeless pieces of driftwood depending on the mercy of the current. Our cry was a plea for a future, for a right to live and love as our birthright. There was though a small mistake made in our placement on this earth; we were Jews, and as such we had no rights.

We sat together, cuddled, holding on to our warmth, kissing and touching, drawing strength from one another, and expressing wishes that we knew could not be fulfilled. I remember saying in a small voice, "Why,

I really don't want to die. Life is so beautiful. It feels good to feel, touch, smell. It feels good to think, hear music inside my head, make up little poems, laugh, and even cry. It feels good to feel warm and cold, or to shiver with anticipation of something wonderful. It is not fair to be cut off from all these feelings. I don't want to die!" Ezjel would hold me tight, reassuring me that there was nothing anyone could do. We should hope. So, we did hope, for a miracle.

We were meeting every day, and spending time together until curfew. Ezjel was allowed in the street after curfew due to his job as a sanitary worker. He wore an armband with "Kolumna Sanitarna" or "Sanitary Column" on it, and that would give him permission to be outside the house after curfew in case of an emergency, such as picking up the sick from their dwellings and transporting them to the infirmary. His job also consisted of fumigating the dwellings after the patient was removed to the infirmary. Most of the members of the Sanitary Column contracted typhoid fever. He was one of the few who did not. Many times we came to my house just about the time curfew was in effect, and my father was standing at the door awfully upset that it was so late and I wasn't home yet. (Being outside the house after curfew was also punishable by death.) During all those hours together we exchanged our life stories from the time before the war, which was another life on another planet. We came from different backgrounds, different families, and different schooling experiences. These differences seemed so fascinating to both of us, and they bound us together. We learned from one another, talked, shared our thoughts and feelings, and then talked some more.

We never seemed to have enough stories to tell. Ezjel told me about his experiences in the Zionist organization, his indoctrination in the Revisionist ideas, the battles of factions within different Zionist organizations, the interplay of various religious and political groups in the small town of Chmielnik, with a viable Jewish population of 8,000, where anti-Semitism was so strong that during Christmas and Easter all Ezjel's best friends from school would not talk to him because he "killed Christ." Where people, Jews and non-Jews, were alike in their superstitions and smallness of ideas, where Ezjel had to fight his brother's battles. Sam was a sick child, and as a result grew up with a hunchback. Children as well as adults in that civilized town would call him names, throw stones and try to touch him for good or bad luck. He grew up with tremendous emotional scars. He was a brilliant student, who was gentle and sweet, indulged by his family and surrounded by love, which enabled him to survive the cruelty and persecution he suffered even before Hitler came to Poland.

I learned about the structure of the Lederman family, about their desire to emigrate to Palestine before the war, about sacrifices they'd made for that purpose, about their inability to do so because of the restrictive laws of the British Mandate. The importance of leaving Poland for Jews never dawned on me before the war. I personally was never exposed to anti-Semitism. My school was Jewish, my friends and my family were Jewish. My scope of interest in the Jewish life in Lodz was limited only to school activities and studies of Jewish history and the Bible, which were included in the school curriculum. (By American standards, though, I am better than well educated in Jewish matters compared to most women of my generation raised in non-religious homes.) So, Ezjel's stories were a revelation to me.

Ezjel and his friends from the Revisionist Movement started thinking about some kind of action to take against the Germans. They tried to make connections with the Polish Underground in order to obtain some arms. Their plan was to organize as many young Jewish people in Chmielnik as possible, train them to use arms, and prepare them for the time when the Germans would come to evacuate the Jewish population to the camps. They realized that their armed resistance would be futile. They were sure they would succumb. But in the process they would take many Germans with them.

The young men were sold a few small firearms for astronomical sums of money, for our Polish compatriots were not too eager to help their Jewish brethren. Somehow, this plan came to the attention of the Jewish Elders. Their feeling was that even in the event of an evacuation, some people would still have a chance to survive. They would be deport- ed to labor camps and survive. If there were an uprising, the Germans would likely kill the entire Jewish population. That was their philosophy, and they threatened that if the plan for an uprising wasn't abandoned, they themselves would bring this information to the Germans.

In the meantime, the Germans brought into Chmielnik another group of Jews from a small town in the western part of Poland, Plock, a lovely place where Jews had been living in relative peace and comfort. When the Germans incorporated Plock into the Third Reich, they of course threw the Jews out. They permitted them to take 20 kg of personal belongings per person, and in the dead of the night, in the middle of winter, they shipped them out to Chmielnik. The refugees came during the second winter of the war and were already tired, hungry, and poor. The Jewish community had the responsibility for allocating these people among the already underfed, crowded, and sick population of the town. There was a family of three—a husband, wife, and a little daughter— incidentally also named Gutman, who were sent to our uncle's house. And room was made for them in a corner of the kitchen where Halina and I slept. And that is how life was going on until April 1942.

## RUMORS OF ATROCITIES

If the Germans had left us to live in these dreadful conditions, we would have made it, but even that was denied to us. Toward spring, rumors started circulating that the Germans were "clearing out" Warsaw, Krakow, and other large cities of their Jewish populations. Rumors told of freight cars being sprayed with lime and packed with people and sent to the east. Rumors described how people were given a pound of bread, a bit of margarine and jam, and told they were being sent to resettle and live in the eastern part of the country together with their families. Rumors told that the freight cars were being sent east, but after a few hours were returning empty because the people had been taken to a camp where they were gassed and their fat was being made into soap. Rumors told that this was going to be the end of Polish Jewry.

But they were only rumors, and one did not believe rumors. One could not believe rumors of that kind because it would mean losing all belief in humanity and the future of mankind. That would mean the loss of all hope, and without hope one cannot believe in anything. And without belief and hope one cannot live.

During that time Ezjel convinced me that it would be wise to make arrangements to obtain false "Aryan" papers. He did not elaborate on the scheme, and I did not ask any questions. I had a picture taken and through some connections submitted it along with some money to have these documents purchased. My parents did not voice any objections, since underneath we all knew that none of us had a chance on the "outside," i.e. the Aryan side of the ghetto. It was just done as an afterthought, or a non-thought. What did we have to lose? After I handed the picture and the money over to our friend Szymek Feingold, I forgot all about it.

During that summer, the family that was housed with us, the other Gutmans, received a message from Warsaw that their family had been shipped out east. Mr. and Mrs. Gutman were so unhappy they were crying, wringing their hands in hollow despair. At the end of the day they were left with the question: "They are gone, and now it is our turn, but when?"

Slowly the mood in the whole town was becoming more and more despondent. The weather was magnificent, the sun shone mercilessly, the clouds went about their business of making rain to give life and strength to the fields. The birds spread the good tidings about their renewal of the life cycle. But the Jews of Chmielnik walked with their heads down, their eyes lost the shine and luster of life. They would stop in the streets to chat with friends and neighbors, only to ask futile questions and receive empty answers. There was an air of hopelessness and doom.

During that time, the walks that Ezjel and I took became more desperate. We spoke about the same things over and over again. Sometimes we played games planning our future: We would continue our studies. Ezjel wanted to be a doctor. We were saying things, knowing full well that they were lies. We were saying them just to hear the sound of the words describing dreams that did come true for other young people. That is, for other young people who had a right to dream and make plans, and whose plans had every chance of becoming fulfilled as a natural course of events.

Toward the end of that summer, my sister and I became friends. The times of our silly squabbles were over. We had to grow up; time was running short. Halina was a very bright girl, capable of thinking and feeling deeply, well beyond her 14 years. She wrote poetry, spoke English and German, was good in math (to my dismay), and was very, very pretty. She was tall, by then as tall as I, and very slim and small boned. She had an oval face of an olive cast with little glowing lights coming through on her cheeks. Her eyes were very dark brown, almond shaped, with thick and curly lashes and crowned by strong brows. To top it all she had a head of soft, wavy hair that was light brown with golden streaks. That was my little sister. She was strong-willed, and not as pliable as I. She had a mind of her own and never hesitated to let you know that. As little children we used to fight a lot. I would boss her around and try to tell her what to do. Even in games we played, I was always Robinson Crusoe and she Friday, I the queen and she the beggar. And this caused a lot of friction. Of course, she had no choice, I always managed to pull rank. But now, in the spring and summer of 1942, when she was not even 14 years old, she started commanding new respect for herself, and I gave it to her. She voiced her opinions, and I listened to her. I accepted her as my equal. We shared a bed, and there was no end to our whisperings and giggles. We would exchange confidences, and to my parents' amazement we never fought anymore. How I wish I still had her! She was a valuable person. She was my sister.

I've already mentioned that my mother was a high earner and a very talented woman of impeccable taste. What was she like as a person? Sometimes I think I never knew her. There was always a distance between us. She was always so busy, and in those days parents were not pals, they were parents, and you accorded them respect. My mother was a short woman. I was taller than she when I was 12 years old. She was on the plump side, and had very small feet and slim legs. Her hands were very beautiful and well kept. She had a pretty face with beautiful, expressive eyes. Her hair was very black, as were her eyebrows and lashes. She had a pleasant smile and an understanding mien. She was lively and smart, of inborn intelligence. She had very little formal education, but was an avid reader, and she always teased me whenever I brought home books from the library, saying: "Oh, that, I read it when I was a very young girl. You will enjoy it." I don't know whether my great desire to read was triggered by her gentle prodding, but we used to compete in that field.

My mother's work put her in contact with many ladies, some very prominent in the social life of our hometown. Her clients respected and loved her and turned her into their mother confessor. They would come to her with all their problems. She would advise them the best she could. They would sense her common sense and sincerity. That made her a very valuable person to know. She had a very short temper. She would flare up instantly, get into a rage, and after a minute forget all about it and be as sweet and pleasant as ever. If she made a mistake on a dress, instead of ripping a seam and fixing it, she would rip the whole dress up and buy new material and make another dress. She was as fast as lighting in whatever she was doing. She had no patience or tolerance for anyone who was not fast. She would fire girls who were slow.

My mother hated housework. This hate for housework was perhaps an indirect cause for her destruction. If we had emigrated to Palestine in 1935, at the time when my uncle Shmuel did, our whole family would've survived the Germans. But she was opposed to the relocation in part because of the difficulty of hiring somebody to do housework in Palestine. She was making more money than my father. Dad was managing and investing the money mother was making. To all appearances he was the head of the family and was making all the important decisions. It was only after I grew up and became a mature woman myself that I realized that Mother was playing a clever role. She was the brain and soul behind our household. She was only leading us to believe that Dad was the one making all the decisions. In those days the man had to be the head of the family. The woman's place was there behind him, being supportive of him. And that was how our household appeared to all outsiders.

During that summer, we were all clinging to one another. We had a feeling of impermanence. We tried to imprint all the feelings on our souls forever—for as long as forever would take. The summer drew to an end. Days became shorter and evenings cooler. People were gathering what little crops they had in their tiny gardens to prepare for the High Holy Days. There was a festive mood in town, mixed with dreadful apprehension. People gathered in homes for prayers, since gathering in the synagogue was punishable by death. People prayed for life and redemption from peril. People fasted and raised their eyes to heaven in solemn supplication. I fasted for the first time in my life. Ezjel made fun of me. He did not fast. He felt that in view of what was happening around us it was the most ridiculous thing to do.

On the day of Simchat Torah an announcement was made and posted all over town that on October the 1st all able-bodied men and women between the ages of 16 and 45 should report to the marketplace at 8 a.m. Ezjel had been taken to a labor camp in Podleze, about eight miles out of town in the capacity of a sanitary person. His task was to distribute charcoal pills for dysentery and to bandage sores on the workers' feet. Besides that and an aspirin there was very little anyone could do to help. Jewish workers in that camp were busy draining swamps. This camp had a reputation of being a very desirable place to work, since the draining of the swamps seemed very important to the Germans, who were going to build roads or something.

In our immediate family there were only two people belonging to the posted age group, my father and me. (My mother was 42, and maybe my memory does not serve me right, maybe the ages for women were 16 to 40. Anyway, my mother stayed home with Halina.) My father and I arrived in the marketplace at the designated time to join with thousands of other Jews. People were restless and curious. We felt this would not be the real "Aussiedlung" resettlement, since not all people were involved. This would most probably mean that people would be picked for work, and that was the reason there was no panic. The Jewish ghetto police were keeping order together with the Polish police and some Germans. This whole morning remained in my memory like a picture visible through a haze. All shapes and colors were muted, people moved at a slow, dreamlike pace, and all details are blurred. I only remember that on that sunny and warm, typically lovely autumn day, there were many human bodies standing closely squeezed, getting tired. I tried to look around, and a German approached me with a whip and hit me across the chest with it. I was stunned and in my naiveté I actually felt personally insulted and my dignity abused. This was the only time I was physically touched by a German and although it was a relatively light touch, it remained in my memory as a revolting act. I looked around and saw that people were being picked out and rounded up. Among them were my father and myself. We were in different groups. I was with the women. After, a short while I heard my name called and I was taken out of the group and sent to the rear. I didn't know what happened. I soon found out that my friend Szymek Feingold, who was a ghetto policeman, had me released. I owe him my life, and this was only the first installment on the deed. He proved himself a friend again within a few short days.

In the afternoon, the people who were not taken with the transport were sent home. I was among them. My father and a few thousand others were sent to Skarzysko-Kamienna labor camp. My Uncle Abraham was also taken away, as well as my Aunt Chana's son and her daughter, Esther, who was my age. The description "labor camp" did not sound ominous, and we were not too concerned. We all hoped and believed that as long as we could be of use to the Germans and their war effort, they would not get rid of us. This idea was also a part of their ingenious tactics. The Germans were selecting the most able-bodied men and women, and the rest would be sent to destruction. We did not know it at the time, but this was what was happening in Chmielnik in October in 1942.

With my father, uncle, and cousins gone, I returned to a home that was a skeleton of what it had been the day before and found my mother in tears. She complained that we would be alone again, without Dad, just like in the beginning of the war when he went off to Warsaw. We had a sense that as long as we were together, the family was together, we would always somehow manage. Now, the disintegration of the family had begun. I had a feeling that this was the end of us all. What would we do? What would happen to us? I had no answers to those questions. They were difficult, but in reality they were only rhetorical questions to which there were no answers.

## OTHER DEPARTURES

In the meantime, the Ledermans were leaving. Their friends, the
Zals, a Gentile family, came and took Sam away on the Saturday before.
The Ledermans were afraid that Sam, as a handicapped person, would be
the first to suffer from the Germans. Then on Sunday, Ezjel returned from
the labor camp and left with his parents to follow Sam to the countryside.
Bogdan Zal was a classmate of Sam's. His father came with a horse and
wagon to take the Ledermans out of the ghetto. There was a funny story
about that fateful trip. Old Mr. Zal had come the day before the evening
they were to depart, and Mrs. Lederman was afraid that he might go out
and see some cronies that night. He was an honest, decent man, who
might without thinking mention that he had come to Chmielnik to take
the Ledermans away. This would be dangerous, and could not be permitted.
So, Mrs. Lederman plied him quantities of good, home-cooked food
(soup, about which he talked for a long time), and a lot of homemade
Passover wine. The poor man ate until his belly was full, then imbibed the
wine, and promptly fell asleep until it was time to go. Later that night,
they loaded the wagon with valuables, silver, household articles, clothing,
etc. Mr. Zal insisted that there was room to take a large wardrobe, but the
Ledermans put their foot down and categorically refused. The noise of
this big piece of furniture rattling along would wake up everybody around
and imperil the poor refugees' lives. He agreed and they left as planned.

Before Ezjel left, he came to see me to say good-bye. I automatically asked him where he was going. He said they were leaving with the Zals and told me the name of the village where they lived. Without any conscious effort, my mind registered that information. He said it without really attaching much importance to that fact that he should not have told me of the plan. At that time one did not divulge this kind of information to anyone. Maybe it was fate, I don't know. Anyway, I remembered.

A little while later my friend Szymek Feingold came to the house and told me that my false papers—the ones Ezjel urged me to get—had arrived. Szymek knew that the Ledermans had gone to the Zals' village. He too was acquainted with Bogdan from school, being one class below Sam and Bogdan, and it was common knowledge that the Zals and the Ledermans became good friends during the war. Szymek suggested that I go to the Zals to see if they could help us, too. We had money and valuables to bargain with, and maybe they could find a way to help. I agreed to Szymek's plan, and that same night Szymek found a peasant with a horse and wagon, who, for a large payment, agreed to take me out to the country to the village of Grzymala. I presented this plan to my mother, who agreed to it with tears in her eyes. She packed a suitcase for me and gave me some jewelry and money, which would be handy in bribing someone, if needed. The fact that I had false papers as a Gentile girl gave me a sense of security. It was Monday, October 5, 1942, when I removed my white armband with the blue Star of David, and at dawn left my mother and Halina never to see them again.

# A SOLO JOURNEY

The peasant, of course, knew I was Jewish and took a considerable risk in bringing me out of the ghetto. He could always claim that he didn't know, though. He had examined my papers, and they seemed in order. But deep down he knew who I was. He was another angel in my story.

I arrived at the Zals' house in the late morning hours. I was met at the door by a young girl, Slawka, who was very sweet and pleasant. She summoned the lady of the house, Mme Zalewska, a middle-aged woman of about 45 years. She was a striking looking woman. She was not very tall, but very slim, with prominent cheekbones, piercing blue eyes, and gray hair softly crowning her head. Her mouth was moving constantly, covering ill-fitting teeth. She had an intelligent look, inquisitive and haughty.

She looked me up and down. She asked, "Who are you? How did you get here? Who sent you? What is your relationship with the Ledermans?" And she said, "By the way, the Ledermans are not here. They did come here, all right, but they left. They went to town and waited at the railroad station to be picked up as a family for labor in Germany. I wish I could help you, but unfortunately, we cannot afford the risk of keeping you. We will try, however, to find a way, maybe to attach you to a transport of young Poles going to Germany to work. In the meantime you can leave your luggage here with us and go on. You have false papers. There are a lot of young people wandering about the country nowadays. They are all running away from the Germans one way or another. You can just knock on the first door, you come to and ask for hospitality. You can tell them you worked as a governess, that you come from a big city, which will explain your speech, which is too pure for this part of the country. People do take strangers in. You can help around the house and stay for a little while at each home."

This whole conversation was held outside the house. She did not invite me in, even to offer me a glass of water. I thanked her for her advice, left my things with her, and walked away. It didn't even occur to me to ask why she couldn't take me in for a little while to help around the house.

The standard of living and education of a farmer's family at that time was still very low, and illiteracy was prevalent. Superstition, crudeness, filth, and disease ruled their lives. People lived in dirt-floored, straw thatched huts without plumbing, electricity, and sometimes even without an outhouse. They lived in those huts together with small l ivestock, chickens, pigs and goats. They wore shoes only on Sunday to church. They ate meat only on Easter and Christmas, and when a cow or calf dropped of a disease. From January till June there was no flour for bread; seed had to be saved for sowing. They lived on potatoes and cabbage. This was the world of Polish peasantry and this was the world I was facing now. It was strange, alien and forbidding.

But I had no other plans. The only thing I wanted to do was to make some arrangements for Mother and Halina. (When I mentioned that to Mme. Zalewska she told me that at that moment nothing was possible, but with time we would see. And I, the idiot, took even that at face value.)

I left the Zal house with just my pocketbook, in which I had a change of underwear, a little bit of money (too much would look suspicious), a rosary, a little Catholic prayer book, and of course my false papers, which were my most precious possession. I walked into a lovely, sunny, dry October day in a strange world, not knowing where to stop, which direction to take, which would be the right way and which would be the wrong way. My mind was numb, my thoughts were dull and the outlook bleak. How can I go to a stranger's house, knock on the door, and ask for shelter? This is begging, and I am not a beggar!

It is still a mystery to me how I managed to get to another village. I didn't know the name of that village, which was like any other in the vicinity, I guess. I saw a house that looked clean and neat. I knocked on the door. I told them my false story and asked for help. I don't remember who let me in. They did not ask any other questions. They said I could stay for a couple of days till the round-ups passed (as if they ever passed—they were a continuous menace).

The next evening, Tuesday the 6th of October, 1942, some neighbors came in for a little bit of socializing and gossip. They were very excited and animated. They were talking about how the Germans rounded up Chmielnik and took all the Jews away. They were saying that the Germans drove the Jews in horse-driven carts, and some on foot. Whoever could not walk fast enough, was old or sick, was killed on the spot. The roads were strewn with corpses.

We were all sitting in the main room of the house, which served as the living room. It was a cool, lovely evening. There was a cozy fire going in the stove. The kerosene lamp was throwing shadows on the whitewashed walls of the room, the flames from the stove were dancing merrily tinting the faces of the people gathered around with a healthy, happy glow. I sat facing the fire with my back to the kitchen. The words I heard stunned me, but I could not afford to react. I could not afford to cry out for my loved ones. I had left my home one day earlier with the intention of finding help and returning to my family, and suddenly, I knew it was the end, and I would most likely never see them again. I did not have a mother anymore, and I would never again laugh and argue with my sister. I was very quiet and did not make any comments. The women expressed some feelings of horror, while most of the men were indifferent. Some expressed pleasure that "it was time the Germans took care of the Jews." Someone interjected that once the Germans got through with the Jews, they would take care of the Poles soon enough.

I sat like a rock with all of these remarks bouncing off me. I tried to tell myself: This is not true; it is all a bad dream. I will wake up soon and everything will be as it was before this nightmare started. Mama will be here, and I will finish my argument with Halina over whatever silly things we argued about. But this nightmare did not go away.

For the next four or five days that I stayed with the family, I slept with the girls in the barn on fresh hay (the beginning of October was still very pretty and warm). I was afraid that I might betray myself in sleep, that I might have a dream or a nightmare and cry out. But, looking back I realize that the girls I was sleeping with were young and healthy, and after a busy working day they must have slept very soundly indeed. I also noticed that I was itching all over my body, and especially at the waistline and under my arms. I didn't know what it was. (Much later I realized that it was an acute case of lice infestation, and I had a tough time getting rid of it.)

There was a lot of whispering and "girl talk" in the barn at night. With more serious concerns on my mind, I didn't particularly feel like participating in these conversations. I didn't want to appear snobbish since I was from a big town and a "governess," which meant an "intellectual," but this position also gave me some leeway since the contrast between me and the peasant girls was justified. Actually, they were quite nice. We all shared housework, and food was served and shared in the big kitchen by the whole family together. I can't recall all the members of the family, but I remember that they accepted me as a welcome guest, and for that I was grateful.

One afternoon, the mayor of the village came to call. He was introduced to me and he and the man of the house went together to another room. At that time a chill went through my body. I had a premonition that this visit had something to do with me. After a while my host came in and said: "There are rumors in the village that you are Jewish. I personally could not care less. But there is a law, and I have a family, and I am afraid. Give the mayor your papers. He will have them checked out, and if they are OK you can stay with us as long as you wish. You seem to be a nice enough girl, and you can give the children some lessons. They could sure use some schooling."

I knew all too well that my papers were less than perfect. They were issued by a village clerk in a false name and would not stand up to a thorough scrutiny. I knew that if they were checked there would be trouble. And I also knew that if I didn't hand over the documents they would have a reason to take me to the Germans, and the mayor looked as if he would do that with pleasure. But maybe giving up my papers could buy some time to go back to the Zals to ask for help.

So I put on a big, brave smile, extended my hand with the papers, and said to the mayor (not a very friendly man) with more bravura than I felt: "Please, here are my papers. Have them checked out as you wish. But I am telling you they are fine."

He took the papers and left. After a little while, when I calmed down a bit, I told my hosts that I appreciated their kindness and hospitality, but I would not abuse it and better leave. They appeared to be sad; maybe they knew that I was Jewish and really felt bad for me. They wished me luck and took me to the gate of the house. I looked back at them standing there, waving. I was cold and didn't feel like crying. Somehow it seemed that this was the watershed moment. From then on, I knew I was on my own and there was no one I could rely on. I was all alone in the whole world. My Daddy was taken away to a camp, and my Mommy and sister were taken away to be killed. I would most likely wind up where they were eventually. But I did not want to die. I wanted to live. I hadn't lived yet. I wanted a chance to live. And maybe, maybe, there was a possibility that they were not killed and they would be back. I had to survive and wait for them.

I thought all these sad thoughts and walked along. It was getting dark, and I passed a house where I saw two men doing something behind a picket fence. As they stood up, I saw that their arms were smeared with blood up to the elbows. What a feeling! Fear and dread! I passed by that house quickly. Later, I figured out that they must have slaughtered a pig in the evening, so that the Germans would not catch them. I met some people on the road and asked them the way to Grzymala, and they showed me. In the meantime the night fell suddenly, as it customarily does in

October. I still don't know how I found the Zals' house, but I did. I recognized it and came up to the window. I rapped on the glass and softly called out, "Slawka." She heard me and came out to see who it was at the window in the dark. How great was her astonishment when she saw me. She put her finger to her lips and made me wait. There were some strangers in the house. I waited.

After a little while Slawka returned and bade me to come in to the house. She ushered me into the main room, where Mme. Zalewska, Jan Zal, who was the man of the house, and Bogdan were gathered all around the table. A carbide lamp was lit, and the room looked warm, cozy, and safe. It seemed to me like a safe haven, and I was loath to leave. I hoped that now at this moment my fate would be decided and by some miracle all my troubles would end and a solution would be found to my misfortune.

The hosts greeted me coolly, made me sit at the table, and have some food. I gratefully accepted their hospitality and told them my story. I described the happenings of the previous days in the minutest detail, and finished with a pleading gesture of helplessness and a question: "Could you please help me? I don't know what to do. I have no place to go. I don't know anyone anywhere. What should I do?"

They listened patiently, and then Jan said: "We may have to find a way to help you. In the meantime we will have to get your papers back from the mayor of that village. The papers are not good, and if there is an investigation, the clerk who issued them may get into a lot of trouble. We have connections with the Underground and will be able to get these documents back. After that we will try to get you in with a transport of young Poles going to Germany to work. That's what the Ledermans did. Don't worry, Miss. As a matter, of fact we have worked out a temporary plan. Bogdan will take you to the forest, where you will stay overnight. We cannot keep you here now, since someone may have seen you coming in. In the morning we will have a plan worked out for sure."

At that he formally introduced me to his brother Bogdan, who was a younger version of himself. Bogdan was a little older than I, a nice looking boy with a kind and compassionate expression and a face that

instilled confidence and trust. He had good, honest, and kind blue eyes,
just like his brother. I instinctively felt that no harm would come to me
from these people. I trusted them.

So, Bogdan and I left the house in the dark and went to the nearby forest. The most peculiar thing was that I felt no fear. I don't know
whether I was still in a state of shock from all I had been through, or
whether I was just learning to accept the inevitable. Bogdan took me to a
spot in the woods, said good-bye, and promised to return in the morning.

I was tired, very tired, worried, and given to a certain lassitude.
I could not articulate and express my feelings, and didn't even bother to
do so. I passively accepted what was asked of me and followed instructions. I was told to go to the forest, spend the night there all by myself,
and didn't think even to question it. I lay down and covered myself with
the coat the Zals had given me. It was chilly that night. It was cold to be
a Jewish girl alone in a Polish forest on a dark October night in 1942. But
I was only 18 years old and tired, so I fell asleep. I don't know how long
I slept.

I awoke with a start. The night was bright with a full moon. The
black silhouettes of the tall trees were clearly outlined against the moon-
lit sky. I was lying down in a small clearing. All around me I could see a
group of Germans in full uniform, accompanied by the dreaded German
shepherds. They stood silently like ghosts. They looked at me and I looked
back at them. There were no sounds. I felt nothing. No fear, no dread, no
hope, no pain. I rubbed my eyes, not believing what I saw. I looked again
and there was nothing. There was the bright moonlight, and the sharp silhouettes of the trees. There were no Germans and no dogs. My vivid
imagination was playing tricks on me. Now I felt relief and incredulity at
my luck. I took it as a good omen. I thought maybe that meant I would
survive, maybe the Zals would come up with a solution to my problem. I
could not sleep anymore, and I waited for the morning and Bogdan's
promised arrival.

I must have dozed on and off, but I somehow lived to see the sun
rising in the morning. Soon I saw Bogdan approaching with a bundle in his
arms. He came and brought me food, which I welcomed, for I was very

young and had a healthy appetite. But most important was his attitude, the kindness and gentleness in his approach to me. He smilingly told me that the Underground had already retrieved my papers from the mayor of the neighboring village, and it was a good thing, too, because he would not have hesitated to take me to the Germans. His sentiments were widely known and he was no friend of the Jews.

Bogdan told me I would have to stay in the forest for the rest of the day. This would give the Zals time to make firm arrangements to have me join a group for transport to Germany. While this was practically certain, he explained, some small details still needed to be worked out. In the meantime, they did not wish to have me come to the house, for fear that someone might see me, and that would be dangerous. He said I would have to learn to be very careful not to be seen by the Germans as well as the Poles. There were many Polish people who would like nothing better than to take a few Jews to the Germans. This, by the way, was no news to me, since I had seen and felt these sympathies from the days when we still lived in the ghetto. Bogdan also tried to put my mind at ease, telling me not to worry, that everything would be all right.

After he left me alone in the forest again, I felt better and started to let my hopes rise. I don't remember how I spent the rest of the day. After dark Bogdan returned with some food again and asked me to follow him. We returned to their house but he didn't ask me to go inside. Instead he motioned me to a little barn, or stable, and asked me quietly to go up a steep ladder to the loft. He assured me that things were looking up, and that by tomorrow at the latest we would have a plan all worked out. I accepted all that with gratitude. I realized that all roads were closed to me, and whatever decisions had to be made, I could not be the one making them, and therefore I would have to passively accept anything that would be offered to me.

Slawka came up to the loft and remained for a little while talking to me. She was shy and sweet. I liked her. I was thinking to myself: Here are two girls of approximately the same age, born and bred in different cultures and environments, although the same country, facing one another. One had a future, the other did not. Both girls were young, innocent, full of life, and deserving of the best life could offer. But for the fact that one was born of an ancient race and the other was not, one had a right to live, and the other did not. I did not expect any answers, though. Slawka left, and I was left alone in the sweetly fragrant loft. I fell asleep immediately, scratching away.

In the morning Jan came up and brought me breakfast. He remained for quite a while. He watched me eat, and then he sat there and we talked. I was struck by the kindness and softness of his demeanor. He asked me all kinds of questions about myself, my family, and my background. He tried to tell me that I should not lose hope of seeing my family again. He promised that he would mail for me a letter to my father, whom I knew to be at the Skarzysko-Kamienna labor camp. We also exchanged memories of my home town. He told me that he lived there for some time before the war. He was so nice and pleasant, like a kind uncle. He left the loft after giving me hope and the courage to wait and believe in a good outcome of our plans.

Slawka returned with the midday meal and a little bit of gossip. She explained to me the family situation at that household, which seemed very complicated at the time. The establishment consisted of Mme. Zalewska, Jan, Bogdan and Slawka, who was the 17-year-old orphaned daughter of Jan and Bogdan's sister. This small family lived in an old, half ruined cottage, which consisted of a small hallway with a tiny pot-bellied stove for cooking, a large bright room used as a living room, dining room, and bedroom for the whole family, a small pantry, and a large ruined room. This house belonged to Jan's and Bogdan's grandparents, and was not in use for many years.

The main house, where the rest of the Zal family lived, was located about a mile down the road in the village proper. As a matter of fact that village was called Zalowka after the Zals. Food and produce were brought daily from the parents' house to this old house. The Zals were the most prosperous family in the village, which did not make them the most popular, ones. There was a lot of envy and jealousy. The Zal children were all educated. Jan was an engineer; the next son, Adam, was a professional officer, presently in a POW camp in Germany; next came Bogdan, who attended high school and was planning to continue with his education at the university. There were two other sons Jozef and Stanislaw, and a daughter, Janina, who were working the farm.

After dusk Mme. Zalewska came up and asked me to take all my belongings and follow her. She told me that they finally found a group going to Germany that I could join. (Later, I always wondered why she had to tell me that story. What was the purpose of it? But, with this woman one never knew what would shoot into her head.) I followed her into the house. We went into the hallway, which cut the house into two parts. There was a stairway leading up to the attic with a trapdoor. She lifted the trapdoor and beckoned me in. I followed her into the attic. It was large and dark with a faint glow of candle light drifting in from the far end. I slowly moved into the room, looking around. I was puzzled, not knowing what to expect. All of a sudden I saw some shadows moving in the direction of the faint candle light. I started in surprise. My first thought was that some Gypsies had gotten in there unbeknownst to the Zals. I cried out, "But there is somebody here!" Then I recognized the Ledermans.

I didn't know what to think. I was told that the Ledermans had gone to Germany. In my childish naiveté I believed it. I believed it in spite of the fact that while Ezjel and his mother did not look Jewish, Sam and Mr. Lederman could never get away with posing as Aryan. The whole idea was insane. I still don't know how I could have believed it even for a moment. Now, it all became clear. The Ledermans had been there the whole time, but the Zals were afraid to let me know that. Their lives, as well as those of the Ledermans, were at stake. The Zals did not know me. They feared that even unwittingly I could have betrayed them. They were in a bind. They were afraid to take me in, and they were afraid to let me go. I later found out that they called the Ledermans downstairs for a conference. They presented the case as it was and asked them what to do with me. The Ledermans did not think twice: Here was a Jewish child, an orphan. Where would she go? They told Mme. Zalewska: "Let's take her in. Whatever we eat, she will eat. Whatever happens to us, will happen to her." Zalewska told them that I had no money, but the Ledermans stated their willingness to share their fate with mine.

This was the closing of another chapter of my life. I stopped being the pampered Edzia Gutman. I stepped through a magic mirror and became a ward and member of the family Lederman. At this moment they took over the responsibility for my existence. I was scared, bewildered, and at the same time comforted. I was not alone any more.

## THE BEGINNING OF CONFINEMENT

A long time passed, though, before I became accepted by all the members of the family. Mr. Lederman, the soul of kindness, was good to me from the very beginning. He was encouraging, he talked to me and smiled a lot. I loved him as a puppy loves a kind man for a show of favor. Sam was kind to me from the very first day, because he was incapable of being anything but kind to someone in need. We talked a lot, hours on end. Mrs. Lederman kept herself aloof and did not show me much feeling. Mme. Zalewska would come up to the attic every evening to take Mrs. Lederman downstairs, after the doors were bolted down and the windows were shuttered. With Mrs. Lederman as her captive audience, Mme. Zalewska would spend hours spewing venom about Mr. Lederman, and now me, that I was a hussy, that I was making eyes at Jan (even though Jan was an old man to me, maybe 40 years old), that I was stupid, etc. And then there was Ezjel. We had been so close, and now he did not even look at me. He'd gotten himself into a lot of hot water because of me. First of all he had told me where his family went into hiding, and he had no business telling that to anyone. And because he'd told me, I came to follow him, exposing everybody involved, including the Zals, to mortal danger—danger that was still very real.

I was very lonely those first weeks and maybe months in the Zals' attic. I tried to avoid Ezjel, to stay out of his way as much as I could, while

Mme. Zalewska did not waste any opportunity to make his life miserable. She taunted him, called him names, and in every possible way showed her displeasure. She was also very disdainful of Mr. Lederman and Sam. The only person she tolerated was Mrs. Lederman, who was smart enough not to get onto her wrong side. Mrs. Lederman agreed with her captor in each and every respect, and thus was able to exist in that very delicate balance of power. We were in a very precarious position. Even when we saw that things in the household were not run properly, we had no recourse. We could never complain to Jan. So, when our staple food was devoid of fats, vegetables, and fruits, we had to grin and bear it. There were orchards groaning with the weight of apples, pears, and other produce, but nobody thought to bring us some. And yet, we were very grateful that we were kept in that house, and grateful when we were given a kind word and encouragement. And so, we had hope. We tried half-heartedly to make plans for "after the war." The sole fact that we were making those plans somehow made it seem that those dreams could come true. At the same time, we really, deep down, did not believe that we would make it. The idea of a time somewhere in the future was a nebulous one. In my imagination I could not paint any factual pictures. I could see it only as an indefinite light that could materialize against all odds. But being as I am and always was a great optimist, I would voice a very definite prediction, based on unending games of solitaire, that we would actually survive. My predictions were well received, since they were much more palatable than the alternative.

We fell into an everyday routine. The morning began with our packing away all traces of human habitation. Then either Slawka or Mme. Zalewska would come in, bolt the doors to the outside, and let us go singly into the "empty hut," the half-ruined room on the other side of the hallway, where our toilet (a bucket) was. After that we were given breakfast, which was brought from Zalowka, the little hamlet where the older Zals lived, and where the farmhouse was. After, that we would read, talk, play solitaire, knit, study, and talk some more before our modest dinner.

Fortunately, we were given lots and lots of books to read. All European classics were at our disposal, as well as school textbooks of history, chemistry, physics, and mathematics. We took to this nourishment eagerly, mainly as a means to kill time. It seemed quite pointless to worry about admission to a university, but "just in case," we wanted to be prepared. So, Sam became the tutor, with Ezjel and me as his students. This situation also added to the feelings of hostility and friction on Ezjel's part. He was loath to lend me books, he constantly argued with me, and in general made me very unhappy. He himself was unhappy and frustrated, suffering the abuse of Mme. Zalewska, who could not forgive him or being the reason I was there. His mother did not make much of an effort to make me feel welcome either by quietly resenting her son's "girlfriend." My position was very tenuous and uncomfortable. Of course, time is a great healer and equalizer, and after a few months' time I fell into my new role as the fifth Lederman and participated eagerly in every activity that was assigned to me.

## OUR UNPREDICTABLE PROTECTOR

Mme. Zalewska, who plied her trade as a nurse and midwife in the village and was paid for services in butter, tobacco, meat, and wool, soon discovered that I was an accomplished knitter. This gave her an idea that she could take orders in the village for sweaters and other knitted goods to be made by me, passing herself and Slawka off as the knitters.

I worked very hard by the light of a carbide lamp to knit big heavy sweaters from homespun lambswool for hefty village folks. I was quick and very proficient. She was making a lot of money out of my work. I have to add that the wool most of the time had to be unraveled from old sweaters, wound up in skeins, washed, made into balls, and then worked from. This was a lengthy process in which all of us participated. Mme. Zalewska was also very handsomely paid for our efforts, but I would never have minded that, because I enjoyed doing it, making up all different knitting stitches and patterns as I went along. What galled me was she rarely would think of bringing us a piece of butter or some tobacco to smoke. And that was not too nice of her, but she was a hard person to figure out.

She'd had quite an interesting life. She was born into a very wealthy timber merchant family in Riga. A trained nurse, she had volunteered for service in the Czarist Army during World War I. She met a young, handsome Polish officer, fell in love, eloped with him, and came to live in Poland and become a Polish citizen. She still spoke Polish with a heavy accent that was neither Russian nor German, although she spoke both languages fluently. She had two daughters and a son with her husband, and they lived in Lodz, my hometown, where she worked as a nurse at a hospital and sometimes as a private nurse at homes of wealthy people who could afford her services.

But she was not happy with her husband. He turned out to be a drunkard. At the same time, Jan, who was an aero engineer, was employed in Lodz, although there were no airplane factories in that city. He fell ill with pneumonia and was hospitalized for a long time at the same hospital where Mme. Zalewska worked. They fell in love. She left her husband and children and went to live with Jan.

During the war, when Jan had to hide from the Germans as a reserve officer and a professional, she accompanied him to Grzymala, the small village of his parents, to spend the wartime in a quiet place, which could afford them some kind of security and safety. She became the housekeeper, or, rather, the chatelaine of his "estate." She ran the household and made all the important decisions pertaining to the general maintenance of the establishment.

Mme. Zalewska had fine skin, which she constantly nurtured with creams that she herself concocted. She used butter, eggs, and sweet cream on her skin, and she had the gall to do it in front of us, who rarely saw a bit of butter. She had a habit of always massaging her face and rubbing it with one thing or another. She dressed in my clothes, the ones I'd brought in the suitcase that she generously offered to keep for me on the first day of my arrival. She tried to look attractive, since Jan was younger, and naturally, she wanted to keep him. She was very jealous of him. I was 18 years old, and she was afraid that I would snatch Jan from her, which was crazy.

On the other hand, she had a great sense of humor and was a born storyteller. She would come to our room in the evening and tell us stories, and we would forget everything and laugh to tears. On those evenings, she was just a charming woman with a great gift for mimicry, who made us happy for an hour or two. In spite of her insensitivity and unpredictability, I felt I liked her when she performed for us. It seemed she wanted to entertain us with anecdotes about circumstances with which we would be familiar, and we appreciated that. Mme. Zalewska told us stories about Jewish customs, holidays, family life. These stories were so true, and showed life in a well established, traditional Jewish family, which she knew about because she had once been a "court nurse" at the home of a very wealthy Jewish family in Lodz. Even I remembered the name of the Salomonowicz family from my childhood. They were a very large and colorful family, and since she lived with them for a number of years, she acquired quite an extensive Yiddish vocabulary.

Then one day in the attic, Mr. Lederman was going through the thatched roof looking for something. All of a sudden he came upon a beautiful old Jewish Bible. It was bound in velvet, with a family history and names of children, sort of a family tree written on the first page. These names coincided with the names Mme. Z's family in Riga. The Bible was from Riga, and every newly born child's name was recorded.

We had come upon a great secret. Mme. Zalewska was Jewish and nobody knew. We had to keep that secret in order to keep our lives intact. We put that Bible carefully back where it had come from and never mentioned it to anyone. We were amazed and aghast. But that explained her familiarity with Jewish customs, knowledge of the language, and superstitious desire to cheat the Germans and save the Jews in her power. We compared her with a good milk cow who would give a lot of milk, but then kick the pail and spill it all out. Her behavior was erratic. At one moment she would be nice and charming, and the next vicious and mean. Many things happened during that 22-month period proved the truth of this characterization.

## FROM THE ATTIC TO THE PANTRY

W e spent the fall of 1942 in the attic. It was a large area with a floor consisting of wooden planks and a ceiling of straw thatch. The thatch was torn off in a few places in order to provide us with a source of light and fresh air. There were some removable, loose floor planks where we could crawl into in an emergency, as we did on several occasions. In view of the secluded location of the house, we decided to have night watches in anticipation of raids by the Germans, the Polish Underground, or any unwanted or unexpected night visitors.

During the day there was always someone in the house downstairs, keeping watch by the mere fact of being there. The night watch partners were randomly assigned by Mr. Lederman so that we all shared the duty equally. We whispered through these waking hours at night, exchanging old stories, feelings, and impressions. We played innumerable games of rummy and read by candlelight an untold number of books. The watch turns I had with Mr. Lederman or Mrs. Lederman were spent telling stories of normal times before the war, of childhood growing up, of Sam's childhood illness. Times spent with Sam were full of talk about our respective childhoods, adolescence, and school. I never spoke about my mother or Halina—I was even afraid to think about them—though I spoke about the possibility of my father being alive in a labor camp.

I dreaded the times when I had to stay up with Ezjel, and at the same time I looked forward to them anxiously. He practically ignored me, did not speak to me beyond the perfunctory exchange of small talk. He was still being baited by Mme. Zalewska because of me, and as a young, callow boy, he reacted to her treatment by being mean to me. I cared for him, and I thought I loved him. I was so lonely. I felt unwanted, unworthy of love, existing only on strangers' sufferance. Those nights were endless.

It was very quiet in the attic. Through the holes in the thatched roof the heavenly scent of damp, freshly mown hayfields would drift in, mixed with the magnificent perfume of pine, fir, and oak forests. The only sounds were the ones of cicadas and frogs in a nearby pond. The sky was black-blue frosted with sparkling stars and the milky glare of the moon. All this beauty surrounding my personal misery would just exacerbate my feelings of loneliness and abandonment. I would sit up with Ezjel, trying to ask him why he was so cruel, but somehow I could not open up to him.

And that was how weeks were passing by. Winter was approaching, and it had gotten too cold to stay up in the attic. One evening during his usual visit, Jan told us that the next day we would be moving to an unused pantry, which would be warm for the winter. The pantry was approximately 8 x 10 feet in size. To the left of the door was our favorite old-fashioned brick baking oven. This oven was always warm, and we could sleep on it, bake in it, cook on it, and warm ourselves by it. The pantry also had a potato cellar, in which we built a compartment for an emergency escape hatch.

So, we moved to the pantry and resumed our daily routine. Talk was the main activity and was interrupted by brief periods of reading, studying, eating, sleeping, and holding our night watches. There were hours upon hours spent in conversations, reminiscing, drawing conclusions, making political forecasts, and deciding on the fastest way to terminate the war. We were receiving pretty accurate news about the war through Jan and his contacts with the Underground, and also from the Polish press, which was controlled by the occupying forces. We felt, or rather we thought we ought to feel, that the war was nearing the end, and once the Second Front was opened by the Allies, it was only a question of time. In the meantime, the Russian Army was surrounded in Stalingrad, and the Germans were going strong in the East, nearing Moscow and besieging Leningrad, after having swallowed most of Europe and Northern Africa. The political situation looked grim, but we refused to accept that fact. We were convinced that such evil could not prevail and the Germans would be defeated. Therefore, when the news of the first German defeat at Stalingrad came in, we were jubilant, but not surprised. We were sure that this was a turning point in the war, and it later turned out that we were right. From that time on, slowly, but surely, the German armies were retreating in the East. The only question was who would last longer—the Germans or the five poor Jews hidden in the Zals' house.

The stove in the pantry turned out to be a marvelous listening post. It had a vent, through which voices could be heard coming from the main room of the house. These voices warned us about strangers. Since Jan was the county head of the Underground, there were always people coming and going who were on the run from the Germans for one reason or another, mainly because of Underground activities. We had to be very careful and not let anyone even suspect that we were hiding in the house.

Through that vent we heard of many unholy adventures of the Underground. There was, for instance, the planned raid by the "Freedom Fighters for Poland," who had gotten wind of a group of Jews hiding in the forest nearby. They could not tolerate it and decided to go and "finish the Jews off." To our amazement nobody objected to that idea. Not even Jan, who in our opinion was the kindest of men. (Although he may have kept his real feelings to himself to avoid arousing suspicion.) Somehow, in the Polish mentality the Jews did not count as people. They were dispensable. Maybe their presence evoked feelings of guilt. Or, maybe they could be considered witnesses to what was going on, to the crimes committed by the Poles as well as the Germans. Our co-citizens did not want witnesses to their own little war on the Jews.

Sometimes other raids were planned. The members of the Underground would attack a German military supply train, kill a few German soldiers, steal the whiskey, sugar, and whatever else the train carried at the time, and distribute the loot among themselves. There was a time when we had a ton of sugar, which was priceless on the black market, right in our hiding place. We ate that sugar sprinkled on our stale bread. It was delicious and felt very nourishing. The Zals felt that the sugar stolen from the Germans was just as illegal as the Jews. They might as well put us together.

At one time we heard of a plan to kill a young man who was suspected of having communist leanings. He had also made the mistake of antagonizing Mme. Zalewska. She was instrumental in the pronouncing of the "death sentence" issued by the commandant. This was a kangaroo court. The verdict was issued in absentia, without the accused having the opportunity to be confronted by his accusers or having a chance to defend himself. Other personal grudges were taken care of in a similar fashion. In view of all that, we realized how much depended on our hosts' mercy, and how fickle Mme. Zalewska's likes and dislikes were.

Our little pantry also had a little window, which was 20 x 20 inches in size, and which we prudently covered with a mud paste. It was impossible to look into our room because besides being covered with dirt, it was placed quite high from the ground, over a man's height. Also, it was dark inside, and at night we covered that little window with a dark cloth

We would stand at that window, our only fragile link to the outside world, for long spans of time and watch chickens pecking at the ground, dogs chasing the chickens, cows ambling by, horses being driven to and from fields, birds in search of worms, worms wiggling away from the birds. They were all free; they could do as they pleased, they could search for their own food, defend their own lives. They could fight for their own existence, enjoy the sunshine, and even look for shelter in cold and rain. We could not do any of these things. We could not sleep on the ground, we could not breathe fresh air, we could chase neither bird nor worm; we could neither defend our own lives nor fight. We were not allowed to actively participate in the act of living. We were passively dependent on other people's charity, mood, goodwill, and circumstances. We could only eat food given to us, drink the wisdom of centuries encapsulated in books given to us, and wait for fate to be kind to us.

The furnishings of that little room consisted of a large platform, where we all slept, the three men on one side, and the two women on the other. In the morning we would put the pillows and covers away to erase all traces of habitation. The platform served as a table during the day. There was also a bench containing our eating utensils and books. The floor was stamped dirt. The walls were white-washed wood. To all appearances it looked like an unused pantry, which it was originally.

The bathroom facilities consisted of a bucket placed in the empty hut on the other side of the center hall of the house, which we used in relays only in the morning and in the evening. In case of an urgent need, and if we knew there were no strangers in the house, we were allowed to give our signal: three double knocks, "tack-tack, tack-tack, tack-tack." Then the bolts would be removed, the front door secured, and the person in need would be escorted to the empty hut to take care of the problem. Every evening, Slawka emptied the bucket into the compost pit, and for that alone we cannot forget her kindness. For washing and bathing, water was brought in a jug. We had a basin and "bathed" behind a makeshift curtain. We still managed to keep relatively clean, washing our clothes in the same water with which we washed our bodies. Afterwards we dried the clothes on a line in the empty hut. And by and by, we managed to do the Zals' laundry at the same time as well. During these bigger "washdays" a wooden washtub was brought to our little room, with a washboard and lots of homemade rough lye soap, and an enormous pot to boil the laundry in. We did this job every few weeks, and it would break the monotony. I was the main laundress.

We were in hiding for some time now. Our food was bad. Food for the whole family was being brought every day from the big farm a mile down the road. There was plenty of food, and whatever was sent was done so with the thought that there were five additional people to feed. The problem was that Mme. Zalewska was a dreadful manager. Whatever she had, she squandered. She would use cream for her face, and butter for some other such nonsense. Foods, such as butter, milk, eggs, cream were practically nonexistent on the market. Rations apportioned by the Germans to the Polish population were a half pound of black bread a day with two ounces each of fat, meat, and marmalade a month per person. One could not live on it. Of course, there was nothing allotted to the Jewish population, since there was none by then. The black market was thriving in the cities. In the country the peasants produced the foodstuffs and the Germans promptly requisitioned them. Of course, some cheating was going on. The peasants managed to hide some of their produce, and there was still some food available in the countryside. Our hosts were very wealthy farmers, so basic food was no problem. There was plenty of bread, for instance. The lady of the farmhouse baked bread every week. She purposely baked it poorly, though, so it lasted longer. If the bread tasted good, the field hands would eat it up too quickly. So the bread was as sour as vinegar. But it was bread.

Every morning Slawka would bring us breakfast consisting of a pitcher of milk and some bread, which was inedible on the third day. For dinner, we ate potatoes and milk, sometimes scrambled eggs. For supper we were given bread and cabbage soup (sometimes with potatoes), and on holidays we could expect a very small piece of meat, bones and a piece of sausage. We rarely enjoyed an apple, even when the orchards in season were bending with overripe fruit, and no fresh vegetables. We were not really hungry, but this kind of a daily diet was not varied enough to be adequate. Of course, we were less concerned about nutritional value of our food intake than with the fact that we were lucky enough not to be starving. With our limited diet and lack of exercise we were not in the best of health, but fortunately only I, the youngest and maybe the strongest, got sick with fever for about a week. Mrs. Lederman made butter in a bottle to put into my soup for some more nourishment.

Sam needed a decent diet because he had contracted tuberculosis as a child. Any time we received something with a bit of fat in it, or an extra egg, or something better, we saved it for Sam. We could do without it, but he needed it badly. There were periods of time when we endured strict food shortages, and once when our scanty diet became even more meager Sam began feeling weak. We knew something had to be done, but we could not ask for better food. We could never complain to our hosts about Mme. Zalewska's mismanagement or lack of consideration. We had to find another way. We knew there was food in the house—butter and eggs—but how to get it? We were almost never left alone in the house. There was always an effort to leave someone back to "baby sit" us, just in case.

One Sunday, though, when the whole family left, we quietly removed the bolts from the door leading to the empty hut and Ezjel went "foraging" in the empty house. On his tiptoes, in stocking feet, he sneaked to the pantry and brought back two eggs, a piece of butter, and a piece of sausage. He had cut the sausage at the same angle so it would not be missed. He took about one tablespoon from the crock, and was careful not to leave marks. From that Sunday on, about two nights a week, when everyone in the house was asleep, Ezjel went to steal food for his brother. Sam ate the eggs mixed with milk, and the butter and sausage with the stale bread. We were all hungry, but none of us would dare touch it. The smell of fresh country butter and homemade sausage still lingers in my nostrils. It gave us joy to deny this pleasure of eating to ourselves. It was for Sam.

Sam refused to eat it at first, but we forced him to. Our argument was: "What if you get sick? We cannot get a doctor here, and if you die, we cannot even bury you." So, poor Sam ate it all, sustained his strength, and we all survived. This is the only time I knew of when Ezjel, a man of honesty and integrity, took something that did not belong to him. But, circumstances can force one to do things one never conceives of doing under normal conditions.

## IMMINENT DANGERS

One day there were rumors circulating in the village that the Germans would be coming to look for hidden Jews. Somebody in the village was presumably concealing Jews, and the time had come for them to be found. Mme. Zalewska came in with this news. She was very agitated, and we were speechless. The horror of the situation was unbelievable. Jan didn't want to face us. She came in to us with Bogdan and said: "You will have to leave the house. Each of you will go in a different direction and leave this area. After things quiet down you will return."

We just looked at one another without any words. What was there to say? We could not protest. We could not argue. These people were the masters of our destiny, and we were only helpless pawns in their chess game. After Mme. Zalewska's speech, the enormity and hopelessness of our situation sunk in. But then Bogdan spoke. He looked at Mme. Zalewska and in a soft voice asked her, "Where would Madame send them? Where can they go? Doesn't Madame know that once they leave this house there is no way back here?" Bogdan took a stand at that time for which he will never, ever, be forgotten by this family. He stood up to Mme. Zalewska and made his point. We were not sent out. Instead, we built a coffin-like box under the potatoes in the pantry's cellar, in which we spent 40 days and 40 nights. We could leave it only twice a day:

morning and night to use the bucket and eat something. We lay there in the stench of half-rotted potatoes in the spring, hoping that we would not be found. The Germans did not come that time. They were roaming the countryside, though, and we were afraid that they might come into our house by accident. They were very busy rounding up young peasants for work in Germany.

After a while things quieted down and we went back to the surface of the pantry. In the meantime, summer arrived and it was too hot to remain there. We were told that we could move to larger "quarters" on the other side of the hallway, a half-ruined room next to the empty hut. In that new room we started to build a very clever bunker as an escape route. At the same time we received news that Mussolini was defeated and captured. The end of the war seemed to be within sight. We traced every Allied and Russian victory on the map. Every inch retrieved from the Germans was a cause for celebration and enthusiastic conversations. We believed in the prompt end of the war. We had to believe, since our nerves were worn thin, and we felt that we wouldn't have a chance to survive another winter. We were exhausted physically, mentally, and emotionally.

During that time Ezjel became a bit kinder to me. We studied and read together with Sam as our teacher and with textbooks supplied by the Zals. We read history, literature, chemistry, mathematics, and physics. We were preparing ourselves for a normal life "after the war." The end seemed to be within sight. All we needed was patience and luck. In the meantime, the race to see whether we would outlast Hitler's armies was still on.

One day during that time, we were up in the attic and Slawka was downstairs alone. Someone came running with a warning that the Germans were in the village. No sooner had the messenger left when we heard German voices. The trapdoor opened. We froze. At that moment we realized that our lives were not worth a penny. We saw it as the end of our struggle, as the end of all our hopes, and the end of our existence. We looked at one another, we held our breath, our faces ashen.

Then Ezjel got up soundlessly and reached for the long butcher knife, which he had honed to surgical sharpness and kept hidden in the thatch in the roof. He took it slowly and quietly moved toward the trap-door. At the same time we heard the ladder leading to the attic creaking under heavy steps. As we sat there with bated breath, we saw a tip of a rifle slowly appear through the trapdoor. At the same time we heard Mme. Zalewska come into the house. She must have grasped the danger of the situation immediately. With incredibly quick reflexes she cheerfully greeted the German soldier in her perfect German. She offered him a drink of Schnapps, which he gratefully accepted. He had innocently tried to come up to the attic, since he hadn't seen anyone in the house. He had been sent with a group of soldiers not to look for Jews but to requisition food for the army. But for the alertness of Mme. Z. the five of us would have perished in no time, together with the family who sheltered us.

We had another near-calamity in the same attic. I think it was on a Sunday. The Zals were entertaining some friends in the main room. One of these men left the room for some reason or other. All of a sudden a squirrel came in from the outside and scampered along the hallway. The young man ran after the squirrel, which proceeded to scoot up the ladder to the attic. The young man in pursuit opened the trapdoor a little bit. But since his eyes were accustomed to bright sunshine, he did not see anything in the attic, which was much darker. Someone from the Zal family immediately came to the hallway and called him down, making light of the whole situation. It ended in much laughter coming from downstairs, and our hearts resumed beating normally. These little vignettes did not add much to our health, but hardened our resolve that every precaution had to be taken to ensure our safety. And that is when the time came to build a bunker, a real one. We set to that task with great energy and zeal. Mr. Lederman was a very good architect and together with Sam figured out the best way to do things. Ezjel was strong and could do the physical work with more ease than anyone else. We women could also carry dirt and dig.

I will not go into detail of how that bunker was built, but it was very cleverly engineered and disguised. It was dug underneath the floor-boards with a little tunnel leading to a hole in the ground that was approximately 61 x 81 inches, and about 4 feet deep. This hole had a tiny window leading to the outside garden, and an air pipe going into it. When we entered that bunker at night, we could close the little tunnel with dirt and bury ourselves in the hole. The dirt in the tunnel could fool dogs if necessary, since it would cover the scent. Just to make sure that the dogs would not find us, we put cages with beautiful angora rabbits on the top of the entrance to the tunnel. This ruse was put to the test.

One day the Germans came in and searched the house. Apparently they had noticed the little matzos that Mrs. Lederman was baking for Mme. Zalewska and suspected hidden Jews. They had dogs, but they did not find us. Leaving, the Germans shot five chickens. Zalewska, in her superstitious way, claimed that these were sacrifices for the five Jews she was hiding. (Among ourselves we were talking about her being Jewish, and that this would be considered a case of a scapegoat of biblical times, according to Jewish lore.)

As before when we felt endangered, we fell into a routine of spending days on the outside and nights in the bunker. During the days we impatiently traced the news from the fronts. We were aware of every inch of progress made by the Allied Armies in Africa and Italy, and every mile of progress achieved by the Russian Armies. And this was no exaggeration: The Allies moved in inches and yards (as for instance at Monte Casino), and the Russians moved rapidly through the plains of Europe. Every new city from which the Germans retreated was featured on our maps, celebrating a new expression of hope. We felt that our stock was rising. Although our incarceration was becoming more and more tedious, the daily routine more and more difficult to follow, and the tempers getting shorter and shorter, we felt that we could have hope and that the time of the German occupation was coming to an end. We only hoped that nothing extraordinary would happen, that the Zals wouldn't become discouraged. There was an old saying—gallows humor—we'd heard back in the ghetto. It said that the Germans would surely lose the war, but the question was whether the Jews would last long enough to see it.

# LIBERATION

It was August the 3rd, 1944, when the Russians, our liberators, arrived. But now what? How to get out of the Zals' house? How to leave the house without tipping off the neighbors to the fact that five Jews had been hidden there throughout a 22-month period? How to sneak out without exposing the Zals to the response of their neighbors, who considered it a crime to harbor Jews? This was no imaginary danger. We understood full well that if the neighbors found out about us the Zals would come to harm.

Then we heard a cry coming from the outside. Someone was warning the family that Bogdan was going to be taken in by the Russians for questioning. From previous experiences, we knew that questioning could only mean one thing: arrest. Arrest would mean deportation, incarceration, or execution. Within seconds Bogdan went into hiding. We did not know what to think.

The general geography of the village was an important factor in the situation. The house we were hidden in was slightly out of the village. The main house, where the senior Zals lived, and where the fields, orchards, and hub of the farm were, was located in the village proper, about one mile away. The main farmhouse consisted of a substantial building, located upon a slight elevation with an unobstructed view of the area. An excellent location for army headquarters. And so, the Russian army decided to use that house as their headquarters. They made them-selves quite comfortable there.

In the meantime, someone not too friendly to the Zals had whis-pered into someone's ear that Bogdan Zal was in possession of a radio. This was forbidden and was punishable by death. Bogdan did in fact own a little radio receiver powered by a crystal. It was a very primitive appli-ance, but it came in handy during the occupation because it brought some news broadcasts. Anyway, this situation was quite dangerous, and we were all aware of it. Mme. Zalewska came running to our hiding place (since we still could not leave the house, we stayed indoors, although not as strictly hidden as before). She cried out in despair: "What are we going to do? The Russians are going to take Bogdan away and kill him! We have to do something!" I mentioned before that Mme. Zalewska was fluent in both German and Russian. It was our mutual idea to go to the Russians at the headquarters and try to talk to the officer in charge and explain the general situation.

Ezjel was elected to go with Mme. Zalewska. He would present the case, and she would interpret. They left and we stayed at the house with great apprehension. Bogdan and Jan had left the house, Slawka was left behind walking around like a lost soul, and we could hardly speak to one another, not knowing what to anticipate.

After a while we heard noises outside. Mme. Zalewska arrived with Ezjel and a Russian officer, with another trailing behind. They came into the house, bolting the door behind her. We noticed that the officer was slightly taken aback as Mme. Zalewska pointed to us and said, "Look, these are the people we were talking about." Imagine what the Russian officer saw: five human figures dressed in peculiar garments with patches in all colors of the rainbow. Five pale, pasty-faced people wearing expres-sions of fear and uncertainty. In their eyes the expression of hope mingled with despair.

The officer could hardly believe his eyes. His reaction was incredulity and shock: "Where did you come from? What happened? Tell me, where were you hidden? I want to see all your hiding places! Please tell me the whole story!" He immediately ordered Bogdan and Jan, if found, to be freed and canceled the arrest order. Mme. Zalewska, with the help of Mr. and Mrs. Lederman, who still remembered some Russian from before World War I, retold our whole story to the officer. It turned out that he was a Russian Jew (who did not speak a word of Yiddish) with a warm and generous heart. He was quite aware of the attitude of the Poles toward the Jews, and decided not to let us out of his sight. He ordered his subordinate, Bykov, to stay with us for a while. He would send for us later on, after sundown, so as not to expose the Zals to danger from their neighbors. He planned to remove us from the house unobtrusively, under the cover of darkness. And so it happened.

An officer, who was a captain, took us to his headquarters, which were in another village house sequestered for that purpose. The details of that sojourn remain slightly vague in my memory. I can only recall that the Zals came to "visit" us with their little dog Mushka. The dog was uncommonly friendly to us. That made people wonder. Also, some villagers remembered that the Zals and the Ledermans had been friendly before October, 1942. All that may have looked slightly suspicious to some, but no word was said about the whole situation, since the Russians—or rather, the idea of the Russian army—instilled a great amount of fear in the Polish population. The Poles were historical enemies of the Russians, as well as the Germans. There was a great deal of opposition and resistance to the Russians. But at the very beginning of their arrival the Russian troops behaved faultlessly. They were courteous, and they paid for whatever food they needed. But there was resistance. We knew it, the Poles knew it, and the Russians knew it.

The captain brought us a goose to cook for dinner. Mrs. Lederman made a princely meal out of it, and I remember this was the first meal we ate as free people. The Zals were our guests, and somehow even their personalities took a different aspect in our eyes. They lost the aura of superhumans and came down to our level of common mortals. We spent a few days in that manner. We were under constant caring supervision of our captain and Bykov. They would bring us fruit from the plentiful orchards of Grzymala, they would tell us stories of their families, their home life—which actually sounded like that of every normal family—and their concern about the safety of their families back home. Our captain would read poetry of Pushkin, which we could not even understand, and we thought he took a fancy to me.

We felt so grateful for all the concern he showed us. He was a Jew whose only way to show his allegiance with other Jews was the care and thoughtfulness he expressed in everyday action toward us. He was always looking out for us. Once while we were spending time with him and his associates at the front, he introduced us to another Soviet officer, David. This man spoke Yiddish fluently, was very friendly, and tried to be as helpful as possible. He also gave us a radio receiver so we could listen to the news (in Russian) and to music, which we enjoyed very much. Our captain, though, warned us not to be too trustful of David, since he was a political officer (Politruk), whose first allegiance would be to the Party. This was our first exposure to the political and social structure of Soviet society.

In the meantime the front was fluctuating. The Germans initiated an offensive. One afternoon, as we were sitting outside, we heard sudden cannonfire. To our amazement and horror, tanks were approaching and spewing fire. Then planes flew overhead. We immediately took cover. There was a cemetery nearby, and we cowered, closed our eyes and ears, hid our heads behind tombstones, and prayed. In what seemed like eternity, we were exposed to a rocket bombing. These were the "Katyusha" rockets. After a while (we will never know how long the strafing really took), when things quieted down, we raised our heads and counted them. There were five heads, all right. We were all there, safe and sound. This was our first exposure to dangers other than the Nazi laws against the Jews. Here we were exposed to the same level of danger as all other civilians and military personnel.

Right after that occurrence our captain sat down to a conference with us. A decision had to be made as to what to do with us. It became obvious that we could not stay here under the captain's benevolent protection any longer. We were threatened not only by the hostile Polish population, but also by the vacillating front line. The best idea would be for us to go east, away from the front. In the east there was already a

Provisional Polish Government established in Lublin under the aegis of the Soviet Union with interim Prime Minister Wanda Wasilewska, a writer and avowed communist who spent the war years in the U.S.S.R. In the east there was some semblance of political and social order. Now we only had to find a way to got there.

The Russians would help us get started, and then "God would provide." The most important thing was that we were free. This fact was still so new to us that we really didn't know what to do with it. Till then, no matter how hard our life was, our everyday needs were being met. Our food was brought to us, our housing was provided, and we had very little need for new clothes. We sort of drifted on, hoping against hope for survival. Now the fact was that we had indeed survived. The time had come for us to start making plans for the future, and settle down to a more or less normal life.

The unpredictable Mme. Zalewska, who had saved our lives, let us out of the house with only the clothes we had on our backs, and that wasn't much. I remember that we took a few bed sheets with us, and I used two of them to make two dresses. One was for Mrs. Lederman, which I dyed brown, and one was for me, a white one that consisted of a skirt and blouse. I don't remember exactly the style. I only know that suddenly, circumstances called for me to become a dressmaker—like my lost mother—and that's what I was going to do. The men in our family each had a pair of pants and a shirt. Ezjel's pants were patched with scraps of all colors of the rainbow, since the colorful Polish kilims were the only fabric available. The only good pair of shoes were the ones Mrs. Lederman wore. Mme. Zalewska had taken all of mine, since we wore the same size. Mrs. Lederman's feet were smaller and her shoes too small and narrow for Mme. Zalewska. So, the rest of us had sandals that Sam and I had made with plaited grass soles and uppers made of scraps of fabric. We really did not look very presentable.

The good captain gave us an escort for a short distance, some provisions, and good wishes as we left. We said a teary good-bye to the Zals, Slawka, and Mme. Zalewska. We all knew that if the front broke and the Germans advanced, we would be destroyed. By now it was obvious that the Germans were pushing the Russians back and were probably entrenched in this position. We had to leave and leave fast.

As it turned out, the front line indeed broke, and the Germans advanced and remained there for another six months. We would never have survived. As a matter of fact, there were some other Jews hiding in the vicinity who were either found and killed or who just died of hunger and exposure. The village of Grzymala was burned to the ground. We were the lucky ones.

# AN ODYSSEY TO FREEDOM BEGINS

We left Grzymala without even looking back. Our general direction was east because it meant moving away from the front line and the Germans. Our own feet and the passing Russian Army trucks were our only means of locomotion. Soldiers in the trucks were very kind and frequently stopped to give us a lift. One day we were picked up by an officer and his group. They listened to our story (by then we could manage to make ourselves understood in a mixture of Polish and scraps of Russian). The officer and his men fed us and found accommodations for the night for us in an empty barn. We were amazed—and grateful—to see that the officer posted a guard outside. His sensitivity to our tenuous situation was touching. The next day he gave us some food supplies and tea, and sent us farther eastward.

While walking through country roads and forests we encountered another group of Jews. There were eight of them. They had a horse-driven wagon, and their direction of flight was the same as ours, so we decided to continue our journey together. As we walked through villages, the peasants would come out, look at us curiously and exclaim mockingly: "Look at those Jews! We thought they were all killed, and here they come out like mushrooms after a rain!" This kind of derision was very painful to us. These people had witnessed the most horrible crimes against humanity, committed against a people who had been their neighbors for six hundred years, and they responded with devastating callousness and cruelty. Of course, we could say nothing. This was why the kind Russian officer had posted a guard in front of our barn while we were sleeping that night.

The next day, we came upon another Russian outfit. They turned out to be political officers, the NKVD, and they took Ezjel in for questioning. We stayed outside waiting for him to return. It was a long wait. All of a sudden we heard a shot. Our hearts stopped, and the fear and uncertainty that we remembered so well from the German times filled us. We didn't know what to think and expected the worst. After a long while, an eternity, Ezjel came out shaky and pale, but sound and hale. He had been questioned about why he, a healthy young male, had been left alive by the Germans. Obviously he was a spy, they said, and a German collaborator. They put a gun muzzle to his head and shot in the air. After more chicanery he was let go.

This episode put fear of the Russians our hearts, and gave proof to the idea that not all Russians were kind and generous. We hastily moved on. The next morning we came to the crossing of the river Vistula. The bridge had been blown up by the retreating German army, and the Russians built a temporary pontoon bridge. We had to wait for the soldiers to cross first. While waiting we observed the young soldiers coming from the front. Most of them were slightly wounded, but all were ambulatory. Some had bandaged heads or arms or walked on crutches. But they were singing and laughing, as young boys do. Suddenly one of them left his comrades and came running in our direction. He fell on Mrs. Lederman hugging and kissing her, and crying out: "U mnie tozhe takaya matushka!" (I have a momma like you!) In his rambunctiousness he knocked out Mrs. Lederman's tooth. She was quite upset, but not for long. He was so contrite that we could not be angry with him. This incident only made us realize that these youngsters were homesick and had feelings like any teenagers away from home and exposed to danger.

We crossed the Vistula and continued on. A member of the group we had joined was born in and grew up in Lezhaisk, which was right on the way to Lublin, the destination we had decided upon. He suggested that we stop in his home town, since there was a family home there, where we could find shelter and stay for a while. We all agreed. It was a typical small, sleepy, provincial Polish town. The inhabitants did not give us a very warm reception, but did not display any open hostility, so we felt it was all right to settle there for a short while. A few days later another group of Jews arrived who had also been hidden by Gentiles. We lived a communal life. Everybody contributed whatever he or she could. Some people would go to the fields and dig up potatoes or go out to the farmers and buy produce and chickens. We shared our resources. The most important fact was that we were free, or so we thought.

After a few days of this peaceful life we found graffiti on the walls calling for "Death to the Jews," and "Jews Get Out." This frightened us. Somehow these threats of death and destruction seemed to follow us wherever we went. The five of us, plus a woman named Mrs. Celia Kotlan and her young daughter, Mirka, decided to leave the rest of the group. The others who remained felt that these slogans were empty threats made by hooligans. The townspeople, they believed, were decent citizens and wouldn't let anything happen to them. Two days after our departure the "hooligans" attacked the small Jewish community. A pregnant woman, Mrs. Haas, was killed. A few others were wounded, among them the young man who had family property in town. He lost his leg. Another vignette of Polish brotherhood.

With no passenger trains running, the only way to get to Lublin was in freight trains or on top of freight cars. Our lot was to ride on top of empty bomb shells returning from the front. Fortunately, the trip was not a long one, and on a sunny September afternoon in 1944 we arrived as free, liberated Jews in Lublin.

Till now I have tried to present the facts as they happened in chronological order. I did not mention anything about my relationship with Ezjel. During our confinement, his attitude toward me gradually changed. He became more considerate and warm. We had long talks about the future and thought that if we were fortunate enough to survive we might get married. The whole concept of marriage was nebulous, though. We never stopped to think how we were going to support ourselves, what our future occupation or occupations were going to be, what our relationship to our parents was going to be, where we were going to make our home, and what kind of a home it would be. When I look back now, it is easy to see how immature we were. We thought we loved one another. The stolen moments of kisses and embraces gave us strength and hope, and made the difficult times easier to endure. And our closeness became accepted by the family, and without much discussion it was assumed that we were a "couple."

So here we were in the provisional capital city of New Poland. And now what? We did not have any shelter and had very little money (the three gold coins reserved for the boys' university education), a bag of tomatoes, and a bag of Russian Army biscuits. We did not know where to turn until we found out from some people that there was a viable Jewish Community Center. We arrived there to find a number of other survivors. We still could not get used to the idea that we were not the only Jews who survived the Nazi occupation of Poland. We would meet other Jews and exchange stories and compare notes. The consensus of opinion was that the Poles as a nation would not find this page in history an honorable one. The cases of murder, denunciation, graft, and blackmail by far outnumbered cases of compassion, tolerance, and help. We blamed the Catholic Church for this lack of compassion and help. The priests in small towns and villages were for the most part ignorant, half-illiterate peasants. Their sermons from the pulpit consisted of promises of the good life in the next world, while the blame for the misery in this world was put mercilessly upon the Jews, the Christ killers, money lenders, exploiters of the poor. It was very easy for people to fall into that trap, especially when getting rid of the Jews meant that most of their property could be had for nothing.

We heard of many cases where Jews were taken into a home by the Poles with a promise of hiding and feeding for a proper payment. After the payment was received up front, the Jews were either denounced to the Germans or killed on the spot by their hosts. We heard stories of Jews hiding in villages where they were born and raised. They would hide successfully for a while, and then someone would get the idea that it would be very profitable to kill that particular Jew for the good boots he was wearing, or for the money he may have hidden on his body. We heard stories about Jews of a very tender age clubbed to death just for the profit that could be gotten from robbing their bodies.

Even before October 1942, Ezjel himself had encountered a Jew in Chmielnik being led on a rope by a peasant to be delivered to the German gendarmerie for the payment of 1 liter of vodka and 5 kg of sugar. Ezjel, who was a lad of a fiery temper, and some of his friends intercepted the peasant and got the Jew away from him. Taken by surprise, the peasant could catch neither the Jew, nor the reckless boys who rescued him. These were little vignettes of the "brotherly love" we were exposed to by our compatriots. There were also people like the Zals, but unfortunately not enough.

We met a rabbi in the Jewish Community Center. He gathered people around him and told us a hair-raising story. He told us that at this very moment there were Jews still living in the Lodz ghetto. He did not know the numbers. He knew that the majority of Jews in Lodz had been deported to Treblinka and Auschwitz, but there were still some left. What their fate would be, nobody knew. We were shocked. Treblinka. I knew that Mama and Halina were taken there. I was told that nobody returned from that place, and most likely nobody would. I tried not to think about them. I felt that if I did not think about them, then maybe I would find them just as they were on that fateful day on October 4, 1942. Maybe they survived just as we survived. Nobody would expect me to be alive now, but I was here! I knew that my father was taken to the labor camp in Skarzysko-Kamienna. This was not an extermination camp. I wrote to him on a few occasions, and Mme. Zalewska was kind enough to surreptitiously mail these postcards for me.

All that remained now was to wait. We had to make arrangements for an everyday life, and wait for the war to end. At that time the front line came to a stop about 20 km west of Lublin. That first evening we had to start thinking about some food and shelter. We were told that at the Community Center there were representatives of the American Jewish Community, who would take care of our immediate needs. This part is also slightly foggy in my memory, but since we talk about it quite frequently nowadays, I know that the representative sent by the American Joint Distribution Committee was a man of a substantial girth with a fat cigar in his mouth, who kept his feet on the table. He epitomized everything we'd ever heard or seen about an "Ugly American." This obese man was sent to help hungry people. He turned us off immediately.

# LABORING AS FREE PEOPLE

One day Ezjel saw a little slip of paper posted on the wall announcing that a position of a wood chopper was open at a bakery. He quickly responded. The position was already filled, but the baker felt sorry for Ezjel and gave him some wood to chop for the next day. In payment Ezjel received a tremendous loaf of hot, freshly baked bread. This was the best bread we'd ever eaten in our entire lives. We ate it with the tomatoes, this bread that was the first wages for work as free people.

We were given free accommodations in a partially abandoned school house, the "Peretz House," a building that was dedicated to the Yiddish writer and was supposed to house a school for Jewish children. The government gave this building to the Jewish Community Center for use as a shelter for the surviving Jews, who were returning from hiding places, camps, and repatriation from Russia.

We arrived at the house; the five Ledermans, and Mrs. Kotlan and Mirka. We were shown to a large room, which was turned into sleeping quarters for people regardless of age and sex. We were given new straw mattresses and blankets, and we made this our home for the immediate future. After a few days' stay in the Peretz House we realized that we could not stay there indefinitely on charity. Therefore we applied, as a family, for a job as the janitors and caretakers of the common areas and halls, which included the toilets. So, Mr. and Mrs. Lederman, Sam,

Ezjel, and I took to cleaning and scrubbing. This job, and especially the toilets, became very difficult to perform. But, as filthy and smelly as these toilets were, they represented part of our job, which we took voluntarily, as free people.

Soon after, Ezjel obtained a better job at a warehouse that stored personal belongings stripped from Jews in Majdanek before their detention. There he found a family bible belonging to a German Jewish family; it was bound in blue velvet with silver trim. We still have it. Also there he found a little silver Star of David, which belonged to some young girl. He took it and gave it to me. I cherished it and never took it off. It can be seen in the picture we took a few days after our wedding. I gave this little Star to my daughter Ruth.

At that time we lived in a small basement room, where Mr. Lederman built us a cooking stove to keep us warm in the winter, and where Mrs. Lederman cooked all kinds of soups, which she sold. This way we made a "living." Since the weather was changing and we were not equipped for the Polish winter, especially with our footwear, we set out to the second hand outdoor market to buy shoes. I was the first one to receive a pair. Mr. Lederman's reasoning was that since I was an orphan, he could not favor his children by buying them shoes before me. It would make me feel bad. So, I received the first pair of shoes. I never forgot that kindness. We still had (or rather Mr. Lederman had) a few gold coins saved from the time before our hiding, which were earmarked for the boys' school, but we didn't know what kind of educational options would be available. After all, the war was still on, and the front line was a short distance from the city.

We had to find a better place to live, since the basement room was damp and cold and winter was approaching. Locating a new home was not an easy task, since part of the city was ruined through the war and neglect during the occupation, and housing was scarce. We eventually found a room in the old part of the city at Grodzka Street, in the old Jewish ghetto.

There had been a thriving Jewish population in Lublin prior to 1939, with Jewish schools, secular and religious, and the world famous

Yeshiva, which graduated a great number of Jewish scholars. The old Jewish neighborhood was located in a medieval Jewish ghetto, where the streets were narrow and winding, paved with cobblestones, and the houses were tall and narrow without sewage or running water. The Germans also designated this area as the ghetto during the occupation.

Our new place was a very large room, approximately 30 x 15 feet, on the 4th floor, without a bathroom but with a sink and faucet. The toilet facilities were located in the courtyard. We all slept there, ate there, and cooked there together. But it was our first "real" home in freedom. We cherished it.

Around November we heard rumors that the Provisional Government intended to open schools and universities. A medical school was scheduled to be opened first. As soon as we heard of it, we made inquiries and applied. Sam did not want to go to medical school. His interests were with the sciences, and he decided to wait till the polytechnic would open. Ezjel and I went to take the entrance examination to the medical school, which was to be named Marie Curie Sklodowska University. As we were taking notes I was thinking that I would probably not have the perseverance to go through years of intense study and hard work. Anyway, if Ezjel and I ever got married, I would most likely have to get a job to support us. I put down my pencil, and sat out the rest of the examination, maybe a little sad, but determined.

Ezjel passed the examination and was admitted to the medical school. We were jubilant. He started his classes on December 8, 1944. In the meantime the war was raging on. The Russians came as far west as Warsaw and stopped on the eastern shores of the Vistula river in the Warsaw suburb of Praga. In August of 1944 the Polish Underground started an uprising, begging for help from the Russians. The Russians sat there watching and waiting for the Poles to bleed. They knew that the people who rose up against the Germans were not their friends.

In the beginning of January 1945, the Russians broke through the front line along the Vistula, and from that time on their progress was unimpeded. Warsaw, Lodz, Krakow, Kielce were liberated, as well as Auschwitz with all its horrors. People started streaming back from concentration camps. The sight was frightening. We saw the gaunt faces, the haunted eyes filled with unforgettable horrors, the shaven heads and misshapen bodies of those who made it. They all gave proof to the stories we had heard. We saw these returnees, as well as returnees from the Soviet Russia, who were shipped to the far east, to Siberia. The men were either conscripted or had volunteered for the Army, and there were many women in the forces as well.

At that time, I kept a job in the Peretz House, in the office serving the new wave of Jewish refugees and returnees. I allocated living quarters and distributed meal tickets. All these people were coming through Lublin full of the hope of finding some members of their families alive. They had no personal possessions, they had no money, but the majority were very young and that was the reason they had survived.

I met a variety of people while working in the Peretz House. My heart went out to them. I tried to be as gentle and understanding as I could, appreciating my own personal position as a member of a family unit, with a home, where there was a kind word, where there was shelter and a hot meal. I believed that what these people missed most was not so much the food, of which there was a meager supply, and not the clothing, of which there was also very little, just barely to cover their nakedness. What they missed most was the family, the warmth, the care and concern.

That was why when I found people with something in common with us, like background, education, age, need, I would befriend them and bring them home. They eagerly accepted those invitations, and Mrs. Lederman gladly shared our food and home with them. (That was when our family expression, "More water to the soup, and it will be enough for everybody," took root.) As we were five people in that big space, there was always room for more. I remember I befriended three people from Krakow—a doctor, his wife, and her brother, a lawyer. They were in the Soviet Armed Forces and were looking for someone, anyone, who could tell them something of the family they left behind. I brought them home, where they shared our hospitality. They slept on the floor, and we sincerely enjoyed their company. After a few days they moved on, but unfortunately they left with us a huge contamination of lice. These were enormous lice of Russian descent, and we had a lot of trouble getting rid of them.

Such hazards did not deter us from inviting more people into our home. I brought in a widowed lady, maybe 45 years old, who became an almost everyday guest, especially at mealtimes. One day I met a girl who appealed to me immensely. She was very beautiful, bright, and about my age. Her name was Jadzia and she had returned from Treblinka. She had been married and had seen her parents and husband shot to death. Shot, but only wounded lightly, she lay on top of the mass of corpses. After the graves were covered with a thin layer of dirt, she crept out under the cover of darkness and ran to the forest. A peasant woman found her, nursed her back to health, and kept her until the Soviets arrived. Jadzia moved in with us when she got ill, and left an unforgettable mark on all of us, especially on Sam, who became very close to her.

One by one, three cousins of the Ledermans showed up: Wolf Wygnanski, who returned from a concentration camp; one named Cukierman, who was sent to Siberia and survived in Soviet Russia; and finally Stefan. Somehow, we found room for all of them. There were more straw mattresses and there was always "more water to the soup."

Time was passing. We didn't have much, and we didn't need much. We had food, shelter, and hope for the future. Peasants would bring foodstuffs to the open market, and the people would buy it with the almost worthless currency, or barter. Ezjel was dealing on the black market in foreign currency and gold coins, and made some money. Then when the medical school opened. Ezjel began attending classes and was doing quite well. We grew closer were considered a "couple," although some people thought that the Ledermans had three children, and that I was their daughter.

## LODZ REVISITED

In January, when Lodz was liberated and was opened, I took the train there to seek information about my family. There was a Jewish Community Center and bulletin boards full of little slips of paper with information about people who survived, and inquiries about those who most likely did not. There were lists of survivors, which were amended daily, and very difficult to follow. I found out that my class in the Gimnazjum had the largest number of girls who survived. I got in touch with them, and we exchanged stories. There were all different stories, one more fascinating than the next. Basia Rosenkranz, who had been the best scholarship student in the class, showed up. She did not look Jewish and had been married to a non-Jewish husband who had been killed in the Warsaw uprising. She was left with a little boy.

Sala Bunimowicz, another extremely bright and beautiful girl, survived the Lodz ghetto and Auschwitz. Since she was sent to Auschwitz with one of the last transports, she had the time and opportunity to finish all requirements for the matriculation examination in the ghetto and was determined to attend medical school. (I later heard that she succeeded, but I lost touch with her.) There were two sisters whose parents had owned the most elegant chocolate shop in town before the war, with their own factory to manufacture their chocolates. The girls, Sabina and Eryka, got the store back, opened it, and ran it. They also got back their own apartment, which had been kept intact by some ethnic Germans who occupied it during the war.

I had to start looking for a place for the Lederman clan to live here in Lodz. I registered with the City Hall, and was assigned a spacious five-room apartment in a lovely neighborhood at Aleja 11 Listopada (Avenue of the 11th of November). We furnished that apartment with furniture also assigned by City Hall from a warehouse of furniture requisitioned from the Jews by the Germans. I had my own room in that apartment, which filled me with pride and a sense of ownership, sensations new to me.

Soon Mr. and Mrs. Lederman arrived in Lodz and started looking for something to do to make a living. Sam and Ezjel came too, during school break. The Ledermans decided to go into business selling textiles at a stand on the open air market. They bought some dry goods from manufacturers with the money they saved from Lublin, and they both went into business. They would depart each morning, and I was left in the house to tend to the cleaning and to watch the pot. I could not cook to save my life, so Mrs. Lederman would start dinner and I would finish it (i.e., watch that it did not burn). I don't remember clearly how I filled my days. I guess I spent a lot of time at the Jewish Community Center making inquiries and looking for familiar faces. I was told by some of the survivors that my mother and Halina were taken to Treblinka on October 6, 1942, and that nobody included in that transport returned. I had to come to terms with the fact that I had no sister, and no parents, since my father, after being shipped from the first labor camp to Germany, had probably perished, too.

I would still take slow long walks along the familiar streets, and would look into the streetcars and into the faces of passersby, searching for the faces I loved and missed more and more. I went to our old apartment at Moniuszki Street. It was unoccupied. From what I was told, the Germans kept the American POWs there. Poor things must have been kept without heat in the cruel Polish winter, since they burned up everything made of wood—doors, kitchen cabinets, etc. The apartment looked so much smaller than I remembered it. But this happens when you go back to a place from your childhood. Now I was an adult and the surroundings seemed to have shrunk. Especially the long corridor, where every two years I would try out my new skates on the coconut runner (to my mother's dismay and disapproval). I left the apartment with a feeling of sadness and loss of the past.

Ezjel returned to Lublin to finish the term (it was a trimester system) at the university. In January, Grzymala and most of the Polish territory was liberated by the Soviets. As soon as possible, Bogdan, Slawka, Jan, and Mme. Zalewska came to Lublin, since both the houses in Grzymala and Zalowka had been destroyed in the fighting. The house and all our hiding places had burned down.

Bogdan expressed a desire to enter medical school. He took the test and failed. We took it very hard. Ezjel decided to go to the rector of the university and plead for Bogdan. He went to see Prof. Parness, whom he suspected of being Jewish, and explained the whole situation. It was obvious to Ezjel that Prof. Parness was very moved by the story, and he promised to help. Since it was already too late for medical school, he suggested that Bogdan enter the veterinary school for the first year of basic studies, which were identical, and switch to medical school the following year. It turned out that Bogdan was so excited by veterinary medicine that he decided to remain there.

In the meantime, we all remained in Lodz, and Ezjel had to return to Lublin, where he lived for a while with Bogdan in our attic room. They shared many hours of hard studying and makeshift meals, which consisted of onions, liver, and lard, on the hot plate. They would purchase the ingredients for that meal every day on the open air market. During his stay in Lublin Ezjel met a beautiful fellow student, Izabella Malinowska, now our dear friend, of whom I was dreadfully jealous. Ezjel suspected her of being Jewish, which she indeed was. She had a boyfriend, Michal. After many complications at the apartment at Grodzka Street, Ezjel had to move. The only available place to go was Izabella's. When I heard about that, I got on a train and arrived unexpectedly in Lublin at their apartment. They were surprised, but glad. My mind was put at ease since I saw that Michal was having breakfast (wild strawberries and cream) with them. From then on, we were fast friends. Michal's brother Romek was Jadzia's boyfriend (the girl, whom I bought home some months earlier). I remained in Lublin for a couple of days having a wonderful time, and returned to Lodz assured that my Salek was my own. I loved him and I missed him.

In June or July Ezjel returned to Lodz for vacation. His intention was to return to Lublin to the University, since he got an offer from the anatomy professor of a job in the department. He was an outstanding student, and the faculty had been completely depleted by the Germans. There was a dire need for teachers.

# A REUNION

On August 3, 1945, I left our apartment to go to the corner bakery for bread. As I was leaving the building, the sight of a familiar figure stopped my breath. My Daddy was back! He looked well rested and very well dressed. He was a very handsome man, 46 years old, and did not look his age. He looked tanned, as if he were returning from a vacation. We stood there wordlessly for a moment and then started hugging, crying, and laughing.

His stories were unending. Dad told us about his work in the labor camp. He was fortunate to have a job in a potato chip factory, which was safe to a degree: there were always potatoes to eat, and the factory was warm in the winter. He told us about the time when he tried to send a Gentile worker to Chmielnik to retrieve the buried gold and money in my uncle's garden in order to bribe someone to transfer his brother Abraham to the potato chip factory. My uncle was working in the ammunition factory, where nitroglycerin ate into his system. But the man returned empty handed claiming that there was nothing in the hiding place, and Abraham died along with thousands of other Jews. I also learned that my father had received my postcards and had derived much joy and strength from them.

As the Soviet Army approached, my father's whole camp was transferred to Germany, where Dad worked on the V-2 in an underground factory in Lothringen. He was a strong man and an efficient worker, and the conditions in that camp were a little better since they had workers from all over Europe, not just Polish Jews. My father had a chance to survive. Toward the end of the war he was transferred again, this time to Buchenwald, where he was liberated by the U.S. forces. By then he was emaciated and starved half to death. He had enough common sense and determination to avoid eating the rich foods showered on the survivors by their compassionate American liberators. Many survivors died from eating too much too quickly after being liberated. He lived on milk and cereal for about three weeks and nursed himself back to health. He heard rumors that I was alive and that I had survived with the Ledermans. His desire was to return to Poland and find me. In the process of returning to normal life he had to provide himself with presentable clothes. He went to an abandoned German house, where he found two sets of underwear, a suit, and a pair of shoes, which happened to be approximately his size. He told us that there was silverware, money and jewelry scattered all over. His intent was to take only what he needed desperately at the moment. However, he saw a small bottle of Chanel No. 5 perfume and took it as a present for me.

Those first few days after his return, we never tired of exchanging stories. Survivors from Chmielnik told us that nobody sent with the transport that my mother and sister were on survived. People were taken directly from the trains to the gas chambers. We had to live with that knowledge. The most remarkable thing was that I never dreamed about mother or Halina. I most probably blocked out that horror from my consciousness. And now with my Dad back, I tried to rebuild our lives. I remembered my father as an affectionate man, reasonable, and very fair. He never promised us anything, unless he knew he could come through. But, once he made a promise, Halina and I knew that the promise would be kept. (I think that's something I learned from my father. I was also reluctant to promise my own children anything, unless I knew I could keep my word. My children knew that when I said, "We'll see," it meant no.)

Anyway, as I was talking to my father I noticed that he had changed. He had become detached, maybe even cold and calculating. His experiences in camps, when he had to fight for survival at any cost, made him self-centered to the exclusion of anyone, even me. After a short stay with us he expressed a desire to return to Landsberg, Germany, where he had come from, in order to put his life together again. He saw I was safe with the Ledermans, that Ezjel and I were going to get married sometime soon, and his mission in life as a father was accomplished. This realization galled the Ledermans. They had a little discussion with him to that effect, and he decided to remain with us. So we became six people in the family. The Ledermans took my father into their little textile business, and he did some purchasing and dealings with Ezjel as a partner.

This situation lasted till October, 1945. Then on an evening when everything seemed peaceful and ordinary, our tranquillity was shattered. We had taken a couple from Chmielnik, Hinda Kleiman and her husband, into our apartment. They had returned from a concentration camp and had no place to live. We were giving them a room in our spacious apartment until they could find a place of their own. On this particular evening, my father went out to meet some friends of his, I was reading in the dining room, and the Kleimans were in their room entertaining a cousin of theirs. Mr. and Mrs. Lederman were talking in the dining room. Sam was away, I think in school, and Ezjel was in the bathroom, which was located in the back of the apartment. The doorbell rang, and the cousin of the Kleimans went to answer it. No sooner had he opened the door when a shot rang out, and an armed man appeared at the door of the dining room, pushing Mrs. Kleiman in front of him. He ordered the Ledermans to put their hands up in the air. He didn't notice me. I saw it all like a movie in slow motion. I knew there was a back entrance to the apartment with a staircase leading to the attic of the building. I also knew that there was a police precinct across the street. I quickly sneaked out of the apartment and ran up the stairs and started screaming for help.

In the meantime Ezjel heard the shot and came running to the dining room to see his parents and Mrs. Kleiman standing in front of a gunman with their hands over their heads. Without thinking, he jumped the man, who was startled by his appearance (he was dressed in a semi-military manner). The two struggled. Ezjel was on top, and the bandit dropped his gun, which Ezjel promptly picked up and tried to use on him. But the gun was jammed. Then Mr. and Mrs. Lederman sprang into action, hitting the fallen intruder with a heavy chair and rendering him unconscious. Suddenly two other bandits appeared at the door to the dining room. Seeing their accomplice down, they fled through the window and down the drainpipe. Then the Ledermans and Mrs. Kleiman joined me in the attic. In the meantime, the police—alerted by my screams—arrived to take the unconscious man into custody. The whole episode could not have lasted more than 10 minutes.

The young man who had been shot, the Kleimans' cousin, was hospitalized. He was paralyzed for a number of months, and after a lengthy hospital stay regained his ability to walk. The bandit was a student from Lublin University. There was a list with names of Jewish families found on him. There was a plan to target and kill some families thereby scaring the rest of the Jews into leaving Poland. He was tried, convicted, and hanged. We made a deposition but left before the trial. We realized that there was no future in Poland for Jews.

# THE JOURNEY CONTINUES

Our plan was to try to get to Palestine. At that time there was a Jewish organization facilitating illegal immigration to Palestine by trying to foil the British blockade. The trip was supposedly arduous and risky. Older people were not encouraged to participate in this undertaking. We heard, though, that from the American Zone in Germany arrangements to leave could be made. So, we sold everything we could, purchased a false permit to cross the border from Poland to Russian-occupied Germany, purchased some U.S. dollars and some scrip dollars, which were the U.S. Zone occupation currency used only by U.S. military personnel, and set on our way west, hoping to never set foot on Polish soil again. There were four Ledermans, their cousin Stefan, who decided to leave the military service, my father and me. Stefan still wore his Polish army uniform, hoping that this would facilitate his crossing the border.

After many difficulties we left Lodz on December 16, 1945 and arrived in Berlin a day or two later. The whole city was destroyed. Everything was covered with a blanket of snow, and it was an unusually hard winter. Temperatures were below freezing, with intermittent blizzards. There was no food, and people were living in cellars and bombed-out houses. Berlin leveled was balm on our wounds. The sight of the total collapse of an arrogant regime, which destroyed a large part of

Europe's population in addition to the majority of Jews, appeared to be a partial retribution for our pain.

After registering with the American authorities for refugees, and after being interviewed by a rabbi to ascertain that we were indeed Jews and not Germans masquerading as Jews in order to escape prosecution, we were allowed into the American Zone. We believed that from there we would be able to make our journey to Palestine with the help of the Jewish Agency, an unofficial organization from Palestine that promoted Aliya (Immigration to Palestine) and facilitated illegal immigration. There were strict limitations on certificates of immigration issued by the British protectorate government in Palestine. This government operated under great pressure from the Arabs (whose coveted oil was at stake) to limit or prevent all Jewish immigration.

From Berlin we were helped on our way to Munich, in the south of Germany, where we were taken to the German Museum (Deutsches Museum), a central point of distribution of refugees. At that time, there was constant movement of multinational hordes of people making their way through Europe, mostly from east to west, on a scale that is now hard to imagine. People were trying to flee the Soviet sphere of occupation, they were trying to return to their countries of origin, and in the case of the Jews, they were trying to go somewhere other than their countries of origin.

The United Nations Relief and Rehabilitation Agency (UNRRA) offered food, clothing, and shelter. It was aided by charitable organizations that included Catholic and Protestant groups, the American Joint Distribution Committee (AJDC), and the Hebrew Immigration Aid Society (HIAS). Refugees were promptly stamped as Displaced Persons, who consisted of liberated prisoners from concentration camps and forced laborers brought to Germany from all occupied Europe. Some of these people had no desire to go back home, especially if their homes were now under Soviet rule. Some were forcibly repatriated, among them many members of the Soviet armed forces who wished to defect to the West. Ezjel's cousin Stefan was one such individual. He realized that he had no future in the Polish Army under the aegis of the Soviet Union.

Defectors from the Soviet army were numerous and included many high officers, who found it relatively easy to escape the hated regime.

The DPs, as they were called, were stateless people, without passports, and without a country to claim them. They in turn did not want to claim any country. They wanted to get away for political or economic reasons. We belonged to the faction of the politically displaced, and we truly had nowhere to go. The DP's amounted to hundreds of thousands of people living in limbo, moving from one camp to another. After a while, some order was brought to the general chaos, and new camps were opened.

One of the new camps was in Neu Freimann, a northern suburb of Munich. It had been a village built for workers' families by the Hitler regime. In Neu Freimann, every family was assigned a little two-story, Cape Cod-style house, with a small plot of land on which vegetables, flowers, and fruit trees could be grown. We found ourselves in such a house, sharing it with my father and with Stefan. It was fully furnished and represented the start of a more normal life.

In the meantime, the UNRRA opened a university, and Ezjel and Sam enrolled in the medical school and the polytechnic, respectively. After a few months, Ludwig Maximilians University in Munich opened and offered some places to the DP students. Ezjel and Sam enrolled and became legitimate students at a legitimate university. Tuition was free, and a small stipend was allotted, enabling us to live with the support of the UNRRA and AJDC. Although my knowledge of the English language was rudimentary, I was able to secure a job at the camp's UNRRA office. The pay wasn't much, but it did help.

Ezjel and I started talking about getting married. Mrs. Lederman objected to our plans, either because she felt that I wasn't good enough or because she believed in the old-fashioned custom that the elder sibling, Sam, should be married first. We, of course, did not share that point of view. By then, we were sure we loved each other and wanted to spend our lives as husband and wife, not as the Lederman children. We craved privacy. We longed for times when we could express our feelings for each other without having the whole family on top of us. And we felt that we were old enough to be making our own decisions about our future. My father had no objections. Mr. Lederman thought it was time for us to be married, and of course Sam was on our side as always. Finally, Mrs. Lederman relented.

Our wedding day was June 11, 1946, the second day of Shavuot (the feast of weeks). We invited about 70 guests—friends and some family. With my honest though feeble assistance, Mrs. Lederman prepared a feast. It was a beautiful day at the start, and tables were set up in the little garden, with roses blooming all around. Unfortunately, at about 3 o'clock, the skies opened and the rain began pouring down. We had to move everything into the house for the arrival of the guests at 5 o'clock. While the dinner was held inside, the ceremony was performed outdoors and according to tradition, I had to walk around the groom seven times, despite the pouring rain. My feelings were so confused—happiness mixed with sadness. My mother and sister weren't with me, although my father was. Then, at the bottom of it all, the doubts arose. Did we do the right thing rushing into marriage when our lives were still so unsettled? When the ceremony was over, I became Edzia Lederman. Edzia Gutman, who had been an unofficial member of the Lederman clan, officially ceased to exist. It was a moment that I had been dreaming about and hoping for, and yet when it was finally here, I felt like the same person. So what was different? The fact was that we had a wonderful time with our friends, carefree and happy. We uttered a few words in front of a rabbi, and with that we entered the world of grownups.

We were different from young married couples today in that we were not burdened with financial responsibility. There was no question of rent, taxes, insurance payments, or utilities, and only limited expenses for groceries to supplement the staples provided by the UNRRA and AJDC. So, in essence, we were continuing to "play house," except that we slept in my room and my name was not Edzia Gutman but Edzia Lederman. My status had changed from being a carefree girl running around with a bunch of students, among them my boyfriend, to being a married woman who lived with her husband's family. At that time, Ezjel and I couldn't visualize moving out on our own, even though we could have gotten a part of another little house for ourselves. Somehow, we were so strongly entrenched in our own particular family structure that it didn't even dawn on us to do so.

Our days were routine: Ezjel and Sam would leave home very early in the morning to commute to Munich. We were two kilometers away from the streetcar stop, although the ride on the streetcar to the University was fairly short. They would come home tired in the evening and settle down to studying. It was hard. A new language, a new system of studies, and a shortage of textbooks were just some of the difficulties. Only great commitment and determination would make such a situation bearable, but we had our eye on the prize. With hard work and resolution, we would pave our way in life. We were fighting for our future, though the exact nature of that future was unclear.

As for me, I would take a bus every morning to Schleissheim, about five miles away, where I worked in the abandoned German military airport that had been taken over by the AJDC, an American Jewish relief organization. The hangars had been converted into warehouses that stored food, clothing, and other necessities for everyday life, which would be distributed to the DP camps throughout the American Zone. My position was that of a secretary to the supply officer for the American Zone. It was a great job, affording me an American military uniform, a salary paid in German Marks and scrip American dollars, a PX card, and a Red Cross card. The PX card gave me access to the PX store, where I could purchase American cigarettes, which were at that time worth more than money. For cigarettes one could buy everything available on the market, including the services of a dressmaker or hairdresser. Mrs. Lederman would use these cigarettes to buy meat, fish, fresh dairy products (we were allotted only powdered milk), fruit, and vegetables. With these foods, the talented Mrs. Lederman would create delicious meals that strengthened our health. The Red Cross card permitted me to buy theater, opera, and concert tickets. We would spend our weekends in the Alps in Garmisch Partenkichen, Berchtesgaden, or Bad Reichenhall, where we could go hiking in summer and skiing in winter. We would get up early in the morning and walk to the streetcar in Munich, just a couple of miles south of our camp. Our knapsacks would be loaded with canned food, bread, some fruit, and of course coffee and cigarettes for barter. Then we would board a train for the Garmish Alps that reached to the sky. Covered in snow even in the summer, peppered by meadows full of flowers, with sheep grazing all around, they were the epitome of peace and serenity. All the bad memories were buried, at least for the time being. We'd find a small hotel and take two rooms, one for the girls and one for the boys, and pay with our coffee and cigarettes. Sometimes we'd be crammed in ten to a room, but we didn't mind. We hiked in the most beautiful places on earth with mountain streams of the purest, sweetest water. We hiked, single file, along the steep paths over gorges. We drank in the utter beauty, breathed the pine-scented air, and made ourselves believe that the future held for us this picture as a promise of things to come. Thus, to all appearances, our life at that time in Germany was not bad at all. We were so greedy to appreciate everything and to partake in every activity, as if to make up for all the time we lost during the war.

A year after our wedding, I received a two-week vacation in a hotel in Bad Reichenhall, a ski resort. This particular hotel had been converted by the AJDC into a rest home for employees. We had a wonderful time doing all the silly things young people do on vacation. We met other couples in similar circumstances and formed friendships. I remember a young couple with a baby who was less than a year old. My heart swelled with a desire to have a soft, sweet-smelling baby of my own. By that time, we had plans to head to the U.S., and I figured that if I had a baby in a year, we could arrive in the U.S. with a year-old baby. Maybe it was a hasty decision, considering our tenuous position. But I never regretted it.

In the beginning of my pregnancy, I didn't even believe I was pregnant at all. My periods had stopped, but I wasn't nauseated and vomiting. I was convinced that I had a tumor. Finally, I broke down and told Ezjel of my suspicions, to his great amusement. I started going to a professor of gynecology at the University, and I became a very important person in my family. Everyone was looking after me, particularly my mother-in-law, who saw to it that I ate properly and had enough rest. That suited me fine. I had gone from being barely tolerated by her to becoming a future mother and a carrier of a Lederman child. I was ecstatic about having a baby. I continued to work until May 1948. The baby was expected the first week in August.

In the meantime, the Jewish people were preparing for the British Mandate forces to leave Palestine and for the creation of a Jewish Homeland, which was to be named Israel. Ezjel, along with most of the Jewish students at the University, got in touch with the representatives of the Jewish Agency, which was seeking volunteers to go to Israel to fight for the freedom of the fledgling state. He went to the organization's offices in Munich as part of a delegation of students. The students, who were in their last year at the university, requested one condition for their volunteer service: that if they survived and if a State of Israel were established, they would be allowed to finish their studies at the Jerusalem University and thus become contributing members of the young nation. The answer was a categorical no. Israel, the students were told, would not need intellectuals and professionals. It would need halutzim (farmers), workers, truck drivers, and the like. Some of the young men did go and were killed in battles, while others survived and flourished in Israel. My husband was among the young men who chose not to go. After all, he had a new wife and a baby on the way, and he was less than a year away from reaching his goal of becoming a doctor of medicine. He was brought up as an ardent Zionist, but at the critical moment, he did not heed the call of Israel. I believe he lived with that guilt feeling all his life. He felt betrayed by his ideals.

And so the time of his final examinations approached. In Germany, as I believe in most of Europe, finishing one's courses conferred the title of physician (Arzt). In order to become a doctor of medicine though, he had to write and defend a dissertation. When Ezjel was working on the research for his dissertation, I helped with some of the translations of scientific papers from English to German (I remember something about white blood cells.) And when he wrote the paper, it had to be typed. Since we could not afford a professional typist and since I had already stopped working, I did the typing myself, sitting on a low stool with my legs all swollen. But I did it with joy. It was another step toward our goal.

## THE BABY ARRIVES

On August 14, 1948, I went to the hospital to have my baby. After a short labor, I gave birth to a big, 3,800-gram boy. Ezjel thought our baby was very beautiful. Since I had never seen a newborn baby, and my image of my baby was something that Hollywood dreamed u p, I was disappointed. He had an elongated skull, closed eyes, and a little dimple in his chin. I didn't know what to make of him, but he grabbed my finger in his little first, and I was sold for life. The realization that this little fluff of a human being came from my body and was the result of our love, would grow into a man, and continue as a man, and be a good man was a revelation. My love for that little man had no bounds. As close as Ezjel and I were, this little baby created a closer bond between us.

As soon as the baby was born we were faced with a dilemma: Should we have him circumcised? European boys were not circumcised as is common in the U.S., and we had seen how many Jewish men and boys lost their lives because being circumcised gave them away as Jewish. There was even a cousin of Ezjel's who did not look Jewish but who was handed over to the Germans when some Polish thugs on a streetcar stopped him and pulled his pants off him. One has to understand that the Ledermans came from orthodox families, and for them to even raise the question was evidence of the great fear imbued by the past. After a long deliberation, Ezjel decided that we were "not going to let Hitler win." We had him circumcised and named him Moshe for both of our grandfathers. We registered him as Marcel Lederman to honor Ezjel's dearest friend Marcel Gheinic.

I stayed home to devote all my time to loving and tending to my baby. He was an easy and sweet baby. I nursed him until he was three months old and then supplemented his diet with a bottle and, later, solid food, which we cooked (with Mother's help and experience), ground up, and fed to him. He thrived, as did many other new babies. There was a strong resurgence of pregnancies among the young women in Neu Freimann. We were all young, healthy, newly married, and full of hope for the future. I believe it was a natural drive for revival and a desire to replenish what was lost. You can never replace your loved ones, but you can rebuild your life and preserve their memory in creating a new generation.

Since the baby cried during the night, as babies often do, Ezjel and Sam rented a room from a German widow in Munich, where they could study undisturbed and prepare for their final examinations. It was another step toward our goal to obtain those important diplomas and visas to the U.S.

Meanwhile, we went through many interviews with the American consular, political, and public health authorities. (I still remember the questions about our opinions of the Marshall Plan and the Soviet relationship to the U.S.) Slowly do the wheels of authority turn, which was really to our benefit. We wanted the interview results to coincide with the academic calendar.

The day came when Ezjel passed his doctoral exams, and with honors. We celebrated by going out on the town with the money that Mother gave us, while she stayed home with the baby. We went to a café and had coffee and cakes. We felt happy but at the same time ambivalent. No matter how hard we tried, we could not really imagine ourselves living in the U.S., dealing with problems of housing and food and all kinds of expenses with which we had absolutely no experience. But in my indomitable optimism, I believed we would manage.

While we tried to come to terms with our future in the U.S., my father and Guta decided to move to the newly formed state of Israel. My father believed he would do better trying to integrate into the Israeli community, especially since my uncle Shmuel, whom he helped in 1935 and who had felt strongly about the importance of settling the new state, was there. In the U.S., on the other hand, my father would have to contend with a new language and an entirely alien culture. So, in February 1949 they left, legally, as by then the Israeli government was established and was actively recruiting survivors of the Holocaust. The new government was especially interested in young men, whom they immediately pressed into military service, albeit without much training. Sadly, many of these young recruits perished in the very first battles. Although my father and Guta were not young people (my father was 49 and Guta was much younger), they were Jewish survivors and therefore there was a place for them in the Homeland. My father gave me $200 and left. With that money, we made our first significant purchases as a married couple: a set of Rosenthal china and a photo camera. Such accoutrements helped to give us a sense of being members of the establishment, of being people with roots, people who plan on furnishing their home and beginning a solid life as solid members of a solid community in a solid country.

In the middle of July, we boarded a train in Munich to go to Bremen, where we would take a ship for America. We were on the way to a new life as parents, as lovers, as friends and companions. I looked into Ezjel's beautiful honey-colored eyes smiling with love. From now on, life was going to be wonderful, and we let it show.

Sam took his last exam at the Polytechnic on the morning of our departure and still managed to meet us at the train station in Munich. His diploma was eventually mailed to Brooklyn. Thanks to the Truman Refugee Act, we crossed the Atlantic on an American troop transport called the General Ballou. During the voyage, women with children were allocated officers' quarters. Thus, Mother, Baby Marcel, and I had a lovely cabin with a private toilet and shower and an officers mess with excellent food (I was especially impressed with milk in cartons). The men, on the other hand, were sent down below in quarters for regular troops, which meant hammocks and inadequate food. Our men did not get seasick, but they were ravenously hungry. Since the baby was given a regular portion of food and only ate a small amount of it, we made meat sandwiches for my father-in-law, Sam, and Ezjel, which we smuggled out of the dining room. They ate this food on the deck in some corner, hiding like thieves.

The crew and officers looked down on us, as if we were animals in a zoo. An example of this was the fact that although Ezjel, as a young doctor, was asked to work daily in the infirmary, he was never acknowledged by the American doctors and nurses. For his part, Ezjel did the work gladly. There was nothing else to do, and he felt he could use his newly acquired skills for the benefit of others. But none of the Americans, who exchanged snacks and chocolates with each other, ever though to give anything to this very hungry young man. He was invisible. He was one of "them." That hurt, and we only hoped that this was not a portent of things to come.

Early in the morning, on July 21, 1949, after nine days at sea, the engines just stopped. I was awakened by the silence. I looked out of the porthole. The sky was still dark, but the shore was lined with the lights of New York harbor. It was the most unforgettable sight. I quickly went to the deck, where other passengers were already standing at the railing. Ezjel found me. We stood there waiting for the Immigration officials to come on board, while we looked at the overpowering skyscrapers, at the incessant movement of cars along the shore, at the enormity of this strange new world, which appeared to be beckoning and threatening at the same time. The future seemed full of unknown obstacles, pitfalls, and dangers. Somehow our hope seemed to disappear. Ezjel and I looked at each other with fear. What would our life be like here? Were we strong enough to plunge into the unknown and come out on top? Maybe we made a mistake, Ezjel mused. Maybe we should go back. In retrospect, our tenuous existence in Germany now seemed so comfortable and safe in contrast to this enormous and intimidating city.

Our ruminations were interrupted by the arrival of the U.S. Immigration officers, as well as members of the press. We didn't realize it at the time, but as members of three generations of one family, we were a rare sight indeed. We became caught up in the excitement of the moment and pushed our doubts to the back or our minds.

Aunt Sarah, my mother-in-law's sister, and her husband, Hymie Salzberg, picked us up at the pier and took us home in two taxis. It was my first taxi ride since 1939.

# IN AMERICA

And so it was on the morning of July 21, 1949, that we started our lives in the USA.

Ezjel completed additional residency training at Beth David Hospital in New York, in order to practice medicine in the United States. Sam entered the Brooklyn Polytechnic Institute as a graduate student in electrical engineering. After obtaining a Master's degree, he was offered a position on the faculty, where he remained for rest of his career.

I started work immediately using my still imperfect knowledge of English. Unfortunately, my gentle father-in-law, Abraham Lederman, contracted cancer of the stomach and died after a four month struggle in February 1954.

Ezjel learned he had malignant melanoma in his leg while he was still in training. Once again the shadow of death hung over our heads. Because of his urgent concern to provide for his family, Ezjel chose not to pursue further training to become a surgeon, fearing he did not have much time left to earn. In my heedless optimism, I became pregnant with my second child, Ruth Ann, who was born in June 1954. Our gamble paid off and the cancer never returned after surgery. We moved to a two family home in Brooklyn, with the Lederman parents downstairs, and a medical office in front. In 1958, our third child, Abby Myra, was born.

Ezjel chose to move his general medicine practice to Canarsie, which thrived for 40 years. We moved to a large suburban home in Woodmere, Long Island, with a separate apartment on the third floor for uncle Sam and grandma Minca. As I approached my 40th birthday I decided to have another child. Was it an instinct telling me to at least partially replenish the loss of those horrific years of 1939-1945? In August 1964, Robert Jay was born.

Sam played an important role in the life of our family. Our children were fortunate to grow up in a household with parents, siblings, grandmother, and a doting uncle. Sam was committed to his work almost as much as to his family, and was an acclaimed aerospace engineer. Beyond his childhood health problems, as an adult Sam suffered debilitating lung and heart disease. But he outlived all of these challenges and died of a brain tumor at age 74.

Ezjel's mother Minca lived together with us, and helped to raise the children. She was the Matriarch until her final days, when she died at age 87.

My father Israel Gutman and his wife Guta settled in Tel Aviv, Israel. We all visited and corresponded frequently. I was with my father when he died at age 87. Guta died two years earlier at age 74.

Michael graduated from Brandeis University in 1970, obtained his medical degree from Mount Sinai University in 1974, was a Resident and Chief Resident at Case Western Reserve University where he became an internationally acclaimed infectious disease and AIDS expert. He married Sharmon Sollitto in 1981, who is an attorney. They have two daughters; Claire and Hannah.

Ruth graduated from Brandeis University in 1975, and obtained a Masters in Fine Arts degree from City University of New York. She married David Sack, a classmate from high school. David is a gastroenterologist. Together, they settled in Cheshire, Connecticut, where she works as a Graphic Designer and artist. They have two sons; Daniel and Matthew.

Abby graduated from Brandeis University in 1979, and obtained a Masters in Business Administration from University of Chicago. She married Gary Zarkin who is a research health economist. She has been a prized management troubleshooter for International Business Machines and now for Lenovo. They settled in Chapel Hill, North Carolina and have two children; Joshua and Rachel.

Robert graduated from Yale University in 1986, and obtained a medical degree from Case Western Reserve University in 1990. He is a research interventional cardiologist at the National Heart Lung and Blood Institute of the National Institutes of Health. He married Laura Waugh, an attorney, in 2003. They settled in Chevy Chase, Maryland. They have a son who is named in memory of his grandfather: Adam Eziel Lederman.

We bought a condo in Delray Beach Florida in the 1980s. In 1989 Ezjel had a massive heart attack, followed by a coronary artery bypass operation. This started a precipitous decline in his health. He lasted five years in a debilitated state. He was surrounded by love, care and fear. He finally succumbed to his failing heart on February 17, 1995 leaving me in a state of pain and bewilderment.

One of his last triumphs and joys was the time of Robert's graduation from Medical School, when Michael, his brother and a member of the faculty, handed him his diploma. I watched Ezjel's beaming face and tears in his eyes, and could read his thoughts: A poor boy from a backward Chmielnik survived the war and lived to achieve this honor. How about that!

I lived alone for two years. I accepted my state and was quite content. Physical activities, social and cultural experience filled my days and evenings. Late evenings and nights were something else. I was alone. I had written a haiku poem for one of Ezjel's birthdays a long time ago. It encapsulated all of my feelings for Ezjel.

*Blond hair, honey eyes*
*Head erect, shy smile, straight look*
*Trust and integrity*

*Feelings deep, warmth abounds*
*Your strong hands intertwined with mine*
*Flow your love to me*

*Let wine flow today*
*Let lights glow, let hearts sing*
*What a happy day*

*Small embarrassed smile*
*Wave of hand—deprecating*
*You feel good inside*

*Years of oneness*
*Years of love, devotion, trust*
*All my life is yours*

A year after Ezjel's death I was introduced to a handsome, distinguished looking gentleman. He had a head of beautiful white hair, and the most beautiful kind, blue eyes. His name was Nathan Fintel. He was recently widowed and lonely. His background was similar to mine; originally from Poland, studies after the war in architecture in Munich. We found a lot in common, and a feeling of mutual attraction developed, which evolved into feeling of mutual affection. After some lengthy correspondence and soul searching we both made a decision to throw our lots together. Nat moved into my house in Florida which he filled with art and light. In 2004, we moved together to Chapel Hill, North Carolina, to a senior development, and to be closer to at least one of my children.

Looking back at my life I see a picture which I could never have imagined. We made it to another country, another culture, a fulfilling marriage, and a rich family life. These pictures are moving through my mind like changing patterns of a kaleidoscope. My whole life was one span of growing, adjusting and learning.

I felt our love and marriage were unique, as if nobody else was capable of the depth and strength of feelings we had for one another. Hiding during the war was such an ironic start to such a long and loving relationship. Although it is 11 years now since Ezjel died, I somehow sense his presence near me, and his constant encouragement. Now, at my advanced age of 82 I can say that Ezjel and I created two generations of people who are contributors and givers. We have made a tiny bestowal to the betterment of this world.

Esther Lederman
Chapel Hill, North Carolina
May, 2007

Newlyweds Esther and Ezjel Lederman, Germany 1946

*Top left:* The Lederman
  Family *(from left)*
  Ezjel, Minca, Sam and
  Abraham
*Below:* Lederman
  residence in Chmielnik
*Bottom:* The town of
  Chmielnik, Poland

*Right:* Halina and Esther Gutman
*Below:* Newlyweds Rose and Israel Gutman
*Bottom:* Gutman's apartment building in
Lodz, Poland

*Left:* Israel Gutman and Guta in Israel.
*Below Left:* Mme. Zalewska with Jan Zal
*Below Right: (from left)* Bogdan Zal, Swafka, Mme. Zalewska and Jan Zal

# ADDENDUM BY BOGDAN ZAL

*I asked Bogdan to write a chapter describing the events of the time of October 1942 thru August 3, 1944.*

*I decided to translate Bogdan's writings verbatim, with no corrections or revisions. The following is Bogdan's version of the events in his own words.*

*Esther Lederman*

## IN BOGDAN ZAL'S OWN WORDS

"Hiding for Our Lives," describes the circumstances of the family Lederman hidden for 22 months by the family Zal.

I received a telephone call from Esther Lederman with a request to contribute a chapter of the book describing my side of that harrowing time.

I am 84 years old and it is difficult for me to remember all the details and the chronology of facts.

Before WWII, I attended gimnazjum in Busko-Zdroj, finishing in 1939 with a "small matriculation" – 4th class. Sam Lederman from a nearby town of Chmielnik was my classmate. We became good friends. Sam was an extremely bright student, hard working and friendly, and very well liked by everyone. At the outbreak of WWII in the Fall of 1939 I visited the family Lederman in Chmielnik, about 20 km away from my home in Grzymala. At that time I met his parents and his younger brother Salek (Ezjel). We formed a close friendship. We agreed with the Ledermans that in case the situation for Jews in Chmielnik becomes unbearable and dangerous, due to the new acts of persecution by the Germans, they should feel free to come to our home through back roads and wait out the crisis. They did that on a number of occasions in the years of 1940-1942. They would always return to Chmielnik after the situation became calmer.

I remember exactly that on October 2 1942, the whole

Lederman family came to our home upset that the Germans were preparing some drastic action against the Jews. It turned out to be the total liquidation of the ghetto.

The Germans collected the Jews on the market place and led them to the narrow gauge railroad. They took them to Jedrzejow and from there to Treblinka. After the total evacuation the Germans checked the vacant dwellings in Chmielnik and killed any Jews they found hiding.

My family, *i.e.* my parents, 4 brothers, sister, niece and Mme. Zalewska lived in 2 locations in the "colony." One was in the village of Grzymala, the other one inn the colony 2 km distant. The Lederman family usually stayed with us in the village. All agricultural activities took place in the colony. I, brother Jan, niece Slawka and Mme Zalewska lived in the village. My parents, brothers Jozef and Stanislaw, as well as my sister Janina lived in the colony. Now, a new dilemma arose: how to handle the saving of a family of four Ledermans?

The Germans issued an edict that the punishment for hiding Jews is the execution of the offending family and burning of the property. One was obliged to report any Jews hiding in the forest or other places.

Our family together with the Ledermans finally decided to make the hiding places in the village, in the old house. We had to organize that fact in secrecy so that strangers saw and heard nothing.

In the beginning the Ledermans found themselves in the attic, then in the pantry, under which there was a potato cellar. An entrance to the cellar was created, where a box was built and covered with potatoes.

A few days later Edzia Gutman appeared. She claimed to be a friend of Ezjel who revealed our address and told her she could count on our help. An 18 year old girl, with false papers as a Catholic showed up unexpectedly asking for help. She asked for help for herself as well as for her mother and sister who remained in Chmielnik.

My brother Jan took an active role in the resistance and had influence in the administrative offices of the county. He got birth certificates and ID papers for the Ledermans.

Edzia did not know that the Ledermans were already hiding with the Zal family. She left our home and found shelter in a nearby village. The citizens of that village suspected her of being Jewish and she was afraid to remain there. Under cover of darkness Edzia found her way to our home again and told us that her papers were in the hands of the mayor of the village. Jozef, our brother went to that village immediately and retrieved the false ID, which could not be allowed to fall in the hands of the Germans. Edzia was sent to the forest for the night. The next day, after a conference with the Ledermans it was decided that Edzia will go into hiding together with the Ledermans.

In the evening we took Edzia to the attic. She got frightened that there was someone there, but after recognizing the Ledermans she calmed down and was delighted. Now the family in hiding consisted of five people.

Now, our immediate goal was to keep the fact that we were hiding a Jewish family in strictest secrecy from our neighbors and numerous other people coming to the house. We had activists from various resistance groups! Peasant Batallions, Land Army (Jedrus), National Armed Forces, reporters from underground press, all meeting at our house and discussing policies. Nobody knew or got any inkling about the hidden Jewish family. Salek (Ezjel) showed the greatest initiative in the planning of secret hiding places. A hiding place was dug out under the floor in the empty chamber. The entrance was covered by a box of dirt. Air was being brought through a duct from the outside. This hiding place was used frequently as a result of rumors circulating of German raids.

Germans used to come to requisition agricultural contingencies in grain, livestock and dairy products. They also organized raids to hunt down healthy young individuals for forced labor in the Reich. During these raids the Ledermans were urged to stay in the special hiding places.

In our village Grzymala there were many underground activists. Germans tried to get them arrested. There were raids and searches in homes of people whose names were on the Gestapo lists.

There was a lot of optimism and hope in the underground press, and a large number of these secret publications passed through our home. Salek (Ezjel) was the main commentator of the progress of the war in Europe. He marked the progress of the Allied armies in the east, west and south, as well as in Africa and Italy. Edzia kept writing postcards to her father in the armament factory in Skarzysko-Kamienna. We would post these cards from neighboring towns so the Germans could not trace the place they came from, or who was sending them. It turned out that Edzia's father did indeed keep receiving them, and after his liberation told us they gave him hope and courage to survive.

Days and weeks were passing in expectation of liberation from the German occupation. We lived constantly in fear of the Germans storming into the house and finding the hidden Jewish family. Finally, in July 1944 the Soviet army approached the river Vistula and created a beachhead at Baranow Mazowiecki. The area around Grzymala was freed from the Germans. I clearly remember the moment in August at dawn when the Ledermans alighted from the bunker telling us that they heard Russian language most certainly coming from the Soviet soldiers. There was great joy that finally nightmare was over.

At that time I had a crystal powered radio which I put together, and tried to get some detailed information as to the situation in our area. This radio aroused suspicion in the Soviet military. This was a war zone and it could indicate a secret spy station.

Captain Schneidklotz came to arrest me, but I was in the old house. He took my father hostage and left for Grzymala to arrest me. I managed to hide, since my brother Jozef came to warn me. Mme. Zalewska took Captain Schneidklotz to the Lederman family and explained to him that I could not be a spy for the Germans. I saved a whole family. Captain Schneidklotz saw that the saved family was Jewish. It turned out that he was also Jewish. There was tremendous surprise, greetings, laughter and crying for joy The captain sent his adjutant for food, vodka, and we had a feast. He wanted to meet me and thank me personally for saving a Jewish family. He happened to be the war commandant of the village Grzymala. This was the beginning of a great friendship between our family and the Captain.

It was decided the same day that the Captain would find appropriate accommodations and move the Ledermans. We asked him to do that at night so that the neighbors will not know that the family Zal had hidden a Jewish family. It all happened according to the plan. The next day our neighbors advised us that there was a friend of mine from gimnazjum in the saved Jewish family. We all went to the Ledermans' new quarters. There were greetings and rejoicing that the nightmare was over. We didn't notice that our little dog Pimpus came along. He was the

Ledermans' mascot. Pimpus was overjoyed to see his old friends again. He jumped around, barked and was immensely happy. Pimpus betrayed the Ledermans' hiding place. By now everyone in the village suspected that the Zals saved a Jewish family.

A few days later the Germans started a counteroffensive, which resulted in great battles with tank involvement. The frontline stopped right in Grzymala. All civilian population within a 16 km radius was evacuated to the east. Our family found itself in a village Ruda near Polaniec. The family Lederman was helped by Captain Schneidklotz to cross Vistula in the eastern direction. After many adventures they managed to reach Lublin.

The beachhead established by the Germans in Baranow lasted for another 6 months. The Ledermans found a room for us in Lublin in the same apartment house they lived. They notified us about these accommodations and five members of our family managed to arrive in Lublin and settle there.

WWII was over. I begun studies of Veterinary Sciences, and the family Lederman left for Germany and then for USA. All through this time we kept communications open by telephone and mail. I visited the US twice. I was received cordially by the family Lederman and their friends.

Samuel, my classmate from gimnazjum was a Professor at the Polytechnic Institute of NY, and he extended an invitation to visit his laser laboratory. His invitation had to be approved by the President of the University. He wanted to meet me. He thanked me for saving Sam from certain death. He also stated that Sam's scientific contributions and accomplishments hastened the landing on the moon by Apollo. This helped the US to be the first to land on the moon before the Soviets. Sam never bragged about his accomplishments in the field of science. At home he showed me bookshelves full of papers, articles presented at scientific conferences at various universities.

In 1981 I attended the wedding of Abby, and was presented at a reception for over 150 guests. Then I was thanked and honored for saving the bride's parents' lives.

In summation: Our decision to save the family Lederman was entirely spontaneous. We couldn't stand by and not offer help. We realized the peril our action would bring in case of discovery. The Germans killed everyone caught hiding Jews.

At this time I and my sister Janina on our side and Edzia on the Lederman side are the only survivors. We developed the kind of relationship which is much deeper than any in families. I derive great pride and joy in Edzia's children's accomplishments. Two excellent physicians, professors in medicine, a son-in-law physician, a son-in-law PhD in economics, two daughters, excellent mothers and professional women, two daughters-in-law attorneys, grandchildren good students, and they will most likely follow in their parents' steps. Edzia always tells me that these are my children and my grandchildren, since thanks to me their parents and grandparents were saved from annihilation and were able to create this kind of a generation.

I can proudly state that my family was awarded the medal of "The Just Among Nations", and a tablet was installed in the Wall of the Just Gentiles in Yad Vashem in Jerusalem. I also received honorary citizenship from the State of Israel.

Bogdan Zal
December 2005

Bogdan Zal and his daughter Marysia at Yad Vashem in Jerusalem Israel in April 1992 for the inscription of his family's name on the Wall of the Righteous Gentiles.

*O*n the 10th of October 2007 Bogdan Zal received a tremendous honor. The President of the Polish Republic bestowed the Commander Cross of the Rebirth of Poland upon him as one of the Poles who saved Jews during the Holocaust in WWII.

Great festivities took place at the Great Opera Theatre in Warsaw, Poland honoring 50 Poles as the Righteous Among the Nations. The celebration took place under the patronage of the President of the Polish Republic, Mr. Lech Kaczynski, and was initiated by the Chancery of the National Great Opera Theatre and the Museum of History of the Polish Jews. Ceremonies were attended by members of the diplomatic corps, Presidents of Israel, Poland and members of the State Opera House of Warsaw.

# Eziel's Story

## PREFACE

I have toyed with the idea of writing down my experiences before, during, and after World War II, with major emphasis on the Holocaust, for a long time, but I could not get up the courage to relive those years. Call it cowardice or reluctance to reopen old wounds that have, during the past 40 years, become covered with a thin layer of epithelium, and which could with the slightest trauma become a festering wound.

I must admit that I am paranoid about that part of my life, which colors my views about the perils that my people are exposed to all over the world, especially in Israel. The awareness of these perils—and the fact that people can benefit from learning about history—is one motivating factor that forced me to sit down and start writing.

Another motivating factor was my recent journey to Washington, D.C., for the Gathering of the Holocaust Survivors. There I have seen the Second Generation of Survivors, who are so dedicated to learning the facts and recording them so that people will have the opportunity to learn from the past and thereby possibly prevent any would-be dictator in today's world from depriving people of their rights and dignity, which could then lead to the ultimate deprivation, of life itself.

I have participated in some of the seminars conducted by the Second Generation at the Convention Center. I came away with a sense of reassurance and, yes, pride that from the ashes of the European Jewry a beautiful generation of people—poets, philosophers, musicians, artists, scientists, healers, lawmakers—is sprouting like "mushrooms after a rain." I use this expression in a positive sense, though I first heard it used about us in contempt.

You will have to forgive me my style of writing, which will probably come out as a hodgepodge of words, but I have had no formal training in writing. I have concentrated my years since liberation on my family and profession. This is then an attempt to recollect as accurately as I can my memories and put them down on paper.

December 1992

## THE HISTORY THAT SET THE STAGE

The history of Polish Jewry before World War II and its survival reflexes is not the purpose of my memoirs, and there are many good history books to which one can refer. However, for the benefit of the many people who will likely not take the trouble to study Jewish history, I will try to give a superficial view of the history of my people in Poland, specifically as it influenced my youth and my political views.

The free Poland was established in 1918, following World War I and the Versailles Treaty. Prior to that Poland was divided into three parts by Russia, Prussia, and Austria. The relationship between the Poles and the Jews prior to 1918 was influenced greatly by the occupying powers. On the Austrian and Prussian part, life was apparently bearable. On the Russian side, things were much worse. Though the various problems the Poles faced were created by the occupying power itself, the blame was placed squarely on the Jews. This created tremendous tensions between the Jews and the Poles, and each of them was trying to sway the Russian authorities, mostly by bribes.

With the establishment of free Poland, bands of Poles, some organized, others spontaneous, started persecuting Jews through beatings, pogroms, and outright robberies. Notable among them were soldiers from an outfit of Hallerczycy (General Haller), who exceeded everybody in their cruelty. This was described to me in great detail by my father on numerous occasions when I complained to him about the behavior of my Polish contemporaries in school, who were vicious in their verbal and sometimes physical anti-Semitism.

Poland went through convulsions like any newly formed state. At first, following the war with the Bolsheviks and the so-called Miracle on the Vistula, the Poles managed to incorporate territories that did not belong to them and were inhabited by Ukrainians, Byelorussians, and Lithuanians in the east, as well as the Germans in the west. This created a large number of minorities, the Jews among them.

At the prodding of the victorious Allies and the League of Nations, Poland had to adopt liberal laws regarding the minorities. Described in the so-called Minority Treaty, these laws were on paper only and never practiced.

There were many political parties in post-World War I Poland: the Peasant Party, the Socialist Party (PPS), the National Democratic Party (ENDEC), the outlawed Polish Communist Party (PKP), and various others. They could not get along among themselves, but on one issue alone they were united: anti-Semitism. They had all kinds of plans for the Jews. Some, like the ENDEC, wanted us to go to Palestine and in the meantime tried to deprive us of all means of economic survival. The PPS wanted us to assimilate. The Communists condemned anti-Semitism but did nothing practical about it. The Polish Peasant Party and its leader, Witos, were rabidly anti-Semitic. They and the ENDEC were in the forefront of boycotting Jewish businesses and forming cooperatives in order to eliminate Jewish merchants.

One of the leaders of the PPS, Marshal Jozef Pilsudski, organized a Putch in 1926, after which he formed a party called Sanacja and broke away from the PPS. Since he wasn't a devout anti-Semite, he was considered to be more liberal vis-à-vis the Jews. In spite of Pilsudski's leadership, various anti-Semitic laws were passed and eventually the Polish government renounced its obligations under the Minority Treaty after signing a 10-year non-aggression pact with Germany in 1934. After Pilsudski's death in 1935, Polish Prime Minister Slawoj-Skladkowski came out with the Owszem policy: Kill the Jews? No! Boycott them? Yes!

The Roman Catholic Church came out with a pastoral letter supporting the economic boycott and accusing the Jews of being Bolsheviks, usurers, spreaders of pornographic literature, and promoters of white slavery. It was signed by Cardinal Hlond and was read in all

Polish churches. Numerous pogroms, in such places as Czestochowa, Brzesc, Przytyk, and Minsk Mazowiecki, were the result. They put severe restrictions on the ritual slaughter of animals (Janina Prystor). That was followed by anti-Jewish acts at universities, where Jews were told to sit in ghetto-like seats. The Jewish students refused and remained standing during lectures. The admissions policies to the universities included numerus clausus to limit the number of Jewish students admitted, and eventually some schools practiced numerus nullus, zero admissions of Jewish students.

The Jewish population of Poland was certainly not united in its politics. There were many factions among the Jews, and they were divided into pro-Zionists and anti-Zionists. The pro-Zionists ranged from the extreme left (almost communist) Hashomer Hatzair, to the center-oriented mainstream and religious Zionists, to the right-wing Revisionists, followers of Zeev Jabotinsky, and followers of Meir Grossman. The anti-Zionists ranged from the Bundists (Yiddishists) to the Agudat Israel, a very orthodox group.

Jews were also divided along geographic and demographic lines. The big-city Jew had a better opportunity to earn a living, while the shtetl small-town Jew lived in poverty under the most primitive conditions. When speaking to my wife, Esther, about life in Poland, I often wondered whether we both came from the same country. She lived in Lodz, where her parents were quite comfortable. I lived in Chmielnik, a small town, where life was miserable. It is very difficult to describe credibly that particular part of life to my friends, survivors of the Holocaust, who were living in large cities like Lodz or Warsaw, or Lwow or Krakow. They were able to elect Jewish representatives to the Sejm (Parliament) as well as to local councils. They were able to attend gimnazjum (high school) even if they were not very rich because there were always some scholarships offered by private Jewish schools to bright children.

# A PORTRAIT OF CHMIELNIK

Chmielnik, where I was born, is situated 30 km from Kielce to the north, and 17 km from Busko-Zdroj to the south. This was a region that was called in Yiddish "Melech Evion's Geeter," which translates as: "The Estates of the King of Paupers." The population of the town was about 12,000 people, of which the Jewish population represented about 80 percent. People eked out an existence by serving as artisans— cobblers, tailors, merchants, and mechanics—for the surrounding population of farmers. Some were geese farmers, who were fattening up geese and exported them to larger cities. With a few exceptions the people were very poor and had no opportunity to extricate themselves from that existence for many reasons.

1. The first one was a lack of educational opportunities. There was no gimnazjum in town.
2. There were no opportunities even to learn a trade. If one wanted to learn a trade, you had to find an artisan willing to take you on as a czeladnik (apprentice), which meant to change and wash the diapers of his children, clean the place as well as be a messenger for about one year without pay. If the artisan liked you, he might sometimes show you some generosity (he could hardly afford it).
3. The authorities practiced the most vicious anti-Semitic discrimination. For instance, earning excellent grades in grammar school was not helpful in getting admission and a scholarship to a government high

school. If you were dull and not Jewish you could earn such a place outside Chmielnik.

4. The City council hardly ever had Jewish representation, since elections were held only with a list of candidates approved by higher authorities, who always managed to exclude the Jews from candidacy. The Jews had their own quasi-autonomous governing body, the Gmina Zydowska (Jewish Community Council), which tried to make life a little bit easier by using bribery as a form of diplomacy in removing or blunting the sharp edges of the anti-Semitic decrees.

My family was not a part of the old-timers in town, because my father was from a neighboring town to the west called Jedrzejow, and my mother was a refugee from a town to the southeast called Wislica. During World War I, Wislica was on the front line. To the west of the Vistula were the Austrians, and to the east the Russians, and since the artillery duels became unbearable, the civilian population was evacuated. I remember how my mother used to tell  stories of that evacuation, especially how both sides, the Austrians and the Russians, would stop the barrage when they noticed that people were trying to escape, thus helping them escape. This was, of course the exact opposite of what was happening during World War II. How armies and their leaders had changed in 21 years!

In spite of the fact that we were not a long-established family, my father was elected president of the Mizrahi Zionist Organization. The Jews of Chmielnik were very ardent Zionists of various shades; from leftist Socialist Zionists to Revisionist Zionists. There were even a number of Communists who spent many years in jails for their political activities. All these activities were the result of anti-Semitic policies of the Polish government and people, and the realization that there was no future for our people in Poland under that form of government.

I would like my dear children, who grew up as free people in the U.S., to get a glimpse of the feelings and dreams that we had in the Polish diaspora, and so I offer the following description of the Betar Movement, which I joined. All the political parties had a common goal, for Jews to have the freedom, like all other people, to develop their own culture and destiny without fear of persecution. The Bundists, the Aguda, and the atheistic communists wanted to achieve their goals in Poland by transforming the government into a free democracy. The Zionist groups wanted to create a democratic Jewish State in Palestine. The Betar movement was founded by Vladimir Jabotinsky, a gifted Russian Jew who was fluent in six languages and was a journalist, writer, and poet. He became interested in Zionism after the pogrom in Kishiniev and was fascinated by the work of Theodore Herzl, who wrote Das Judenstaat. He became active in the World Zionist Organization and strived to create an independent Jewish State in Palestine, which he believed could only be achieved through an armed struggle. He was opposed to the popular socialist ideas of that time because of the fact that Marxism opposes the individualism of people. However, he stated that if, after achieving statehood, the majority of Jews chose socialism, he would accept it. His opponents called him a fascist. During World War I, he established the Jewish Legion together with Joseph Trumpeldor. He insisted that Jews must train in self-defense. In 1935, he bolted from the World Zionist Organization because of that body's refusal to define the aim of Zionism as the establishment of a Jewish State (17th Congress, 1931). After Hitler's rise to power, he tried to persuade the European states, especially Poland, to establish a 10-year plan to evacuate 1.5 million Jews from Europe. He was called a traitor by Ben Gurion.

Jabotinsky's followers were the people who originally organized the Haganah and then the Irgun Zvai Leumi, whose goal it was to defend the Jews of Palestine against the anti-Jewish violence of the Arabs and to force the British out. The rest is history.

The political divisions of the Polish Jewry were clearly reflected in my hometown, which was mostly pro-Zionist. During and after the elections to the Zionist Congress, there were numerous demonstrations and even physical clashes between the leftists and the rightists. The entire Jewish population of the town was deeply involved in those affairs.

## LIFE AS A JEWISH BOY

**M**y boyhood friends were mostly Jewish, but I also had some Catholic friends to whom I was very close. One boy in particular, Maciejewski, was a very good friend, and when his mother died he used to spend a lot of time in my home and would have lunch with us, which was the main meal of the day, on school days. What was always so painful to me was that during Christmas and Easter he would avoid me. When I confronted him and asked him why, he said that I had killed his God. During those holidays it was not safe to stray into a neighborhood that was not strictly Jewish.

When I was younger, I was continuously exposed to minor day-to-day incidents where Jewish people were mocked and portrayed in the worst possible light. We were the lichwiarze (usurers) and cheats. We could not stand up to anyone, because we were cowards. We could not fight. Moishe Karabin (Moishe the Rifle) was the epithet for the Jewish conscript.

An incident (one of many) that stands out in my mind occurred during choir practice. We were singing and stretching out the last note, and the teacher, Kuczyski, whom I liked, said, "Don't sing like the Jews in the synagogue." There were times when I actually hated myself for being Jewish, because I started believing some of these lies. Repeat a lie often enough, and in time some of it will become credible.

There were, of course, Poles who did not like to see what was happening and would sometimes utter some words of condemnation of the system. There was a school principal by the name of Gromadzki. He had a mild hunchback and a very fine face with deep expressive eyes. One day he called me into his office and said to me, "Why did your name have to be Lederman? With your ability and grades you should have gotten the full scholarship that I applied for on your behalf but was denied. Instead a mediocre fellow has gotten it. Shame on this government."

There were incidents of anti-Semitism on a personal level as well as organized anti-Semitic activities in my hometown. These included economic discrimination, like boycotts of Jewish-owned enterprises, including small insignificant little shops, which were pasted over with slogans like Nie kupuj u Zyda ("Don't Buy From a Jew"). There were also government edicts that deprived many Jews of a livelihood. For example, my father had a small business. He bought goose feathers and employed a number of people to sort those feathers and pack them for export to Germany, France, England, and the U.S. These were fancy feathers (called in German Schmuckfedern), used as hat ornaments, as shuttlecocks for badminton, and as toothpicks. This export market had been created by a few Jewish entrepreneurs, and although it provided a very meager income, it sustained numerous families. Then came the nephew of the Minister of Commerce, who prevailed upon his uncle to cancel all export licenses. He then obtained the exclusive export license, which resulted in the financial ruin of many people. But Jewish people have learned the art of survival, thanks to many centuries of struggling for survival. The feather merchants prevailed upon their customers in the U.S., France, Germany, and England not to buy from this person, and after several months the export licenses were reinstated to the Jewish merchants.

Other anti-Semitic events included the famous pogroms like the one in Przytyk, where the church bells were tolling in a call upon the faithful to attack the Jews. This happened in 1935 or 1936. In that particular situation, the Zionist youth organized a self-defense group and put all those attackers to flight. Of course, the police arrested the Jewish boys.

The major problem, at least in my hometown, was what the Catholic priests were preaching in the churches on Sundays. I sneaked into a church one Sunday with my friend Maciejewski and listened to the absolute anti-Semitic venom being spewed and how often the priest reminded his parishioners that the Jews killed God (Bogobojcy).

In retrospect, I can hardly blame those illiterate, ill-clad, poor people for hating us. They were continuously being told that the Jews were responsible for all their problems. They walked barefoot to church from their villages and would put on their shoes in the churchyard, right before entering the church. Incidentally, the Polish farmers in our area hardly ever ate meat unless a cow died or a calf was stillborn. They had no meat for the holidays. The richer farmers would kill a pig and have meat for the holidays, and the rest of the carcass would be hung in the barn or in the attic to dry and preserve in salt for other festive occasions. During epidemics they looked with suspicion at the Jews. When they engaged in a conversation about religion with a Jew, they would cross themselves to, in their minds, chase the Devil away.

It would probably sound and appear childish to you if I admit that even later in my years I was very apprehensive at the sight of a cross, which to me was only symbol of oppression and Jew hatred. For example, when I came to the U.S. and was an intern at the hospital, the Catholic priest would come by to give some patients their Last Rites. He used to put a cross on the patient, and I could not even touch that cross during the examination, when I needed to listen to the heart. I would hesitate to nudge it aside. One priest was a very intelligent and perceptive man and he apparently noticed that I behaved strangely. He asked me to talk with him. I admitted to him my prejudice and I told him the reasons for it. He then went out of his way to explain to assure me that the Catholic Church in the U.S. is very different from the one in Poland.

These anti-Semitic actions and the behavior of our Polish compatriots gave Zionism fertile ground among the Jewish youth. Jewish children would never be able to grow and develop according to our ability in Poland. Having realized this, many of our parents, including mine, were trying to get out of Poland. Some succeeded via illegal immigration, some youths succeeded via Hachshara and the Kibbutz movement, but most, of course did not succeed. In the case of my family, my father was trying desperately to get out of Poland to Palestine. The only sure and legal way of doing so was by getting an English Certificate of Immigration to Palestine, the so-called "Capitalist Certificate." In order to obtain one, a person had to have 1000 Pounds

Sterling, which was then equivalent to 27,000 Zlotys. That was a fortune very few people had. Anybody who had that kind of money was probably reluctant to part with a business that had allowed him to accumulate such a sum.

We had an uncle in Palestine, my mother's brother Shmuel, who had a carpentry shop in Petach Tikvah. He promised to get immigration papers for us if we could produce a bona fide Karta Rzemieslnicza (master's certificate in carpentry) for my father. My father sold his business in 1935 and bribed the appropriate agency through a macher, a sort of go-between in the art of bribery, named Szperling, who obtained an official document. Lo and behold, the English decided that they had already allowed enough carpenters into Palestine, and this plot failed. The next plan was to have my father certified as a shochet (ritual slaughterer). Another episode followed, with all kinds of people coming to our home and negotiating terms and payoffs to obtain that certificate. Although all of these proceedings came to fruition at our end, something went wrong on the Palestinian side. My parents used to blame my uncle Shmuel and his wife, Helcia, for that fiasco.

Every time we went through these processes, my parents would come out financially broke. My father had to start all over again in his feather business. Fortunately, with the help of some friends who used to give interest-free loans, Father was able to bounce back and feed the family.

Many U.S. Jews used to ask me after the war why we didn't get out of Poland before the war. I found it strange that so many very intelligent and knowledgeable people in the U.S. have never been made aware of the true facts, that people could not get out of Europe when the Nazis came to power. Most of them had no means to travel and the ones who had the means rarely found a country willing to take them in.

My teenage years were filled with worries and fears. One had to grow up quickly. I became interested in political affairs affecting Poland and Europe. I could not believe that no one could get people together to stop the Nazis. It was frustrating and very alarming when, during the Nazi pressure on Czechoslovakia, our Polish government started pressure of its own regarding a small piece of land called Zaolzie (beyond the river Olza). The government and most Polish people were too myopic in their comprehension of the problem and helped the Germans liquidate Czechoslovakia, thereby exposing the southern Polish border to occupation by the Germans. Once that was accomplished, Poland had the Germans to the west, south, and north, leaving only the eastern border of the country to face the Russians.

Many of the Jewish people were acutely conscious of those dangers and would whisper their disapproval of the policies of the government. I recall how one of our teachers, Kulczycki, was preaching from the balcony of the family Ehrlich in the Rynek (market square) about the cowardly Jews, who did not respect and support the "legitimate" rights of the Polish people to Zaolzie. He was also preaching against the Lithuanians, threatening that "we will cover them with our caps," and they will disappear. The Poles laid claims to parts of Lithuania at the same time. Unfortunately the population, mostly peasant and half literate, went along with these slogans.

## HITLER'S PUSH

In 1939, the Germans started their push eastward requesting Danzig and the corridor across Poland. It soon became obvious that Hitler wanted to subjugate all of Poland. The Jewish people started feeling the pressures first, when the Polish government created a law that revoked the citizenship of all people who had been out of the country for more than five years. This law primarily affected Polish Jews who worked in Germany. In a countermeasure, two days before the law took effect, Germany deported these Jews, pushing them into a sort of no-man's-land between Poland and Germany.

My father became active in what was known as the Rescue Committee, and he and his friends traveled by truck to the German border with food and supplies to help these people. I recall how some of these refugees were brought to our town. They believed that their plight was only temporary, and that the Germans would soon allow them to return to their homes in Germany, since Germans were all civilized people. Some of these refugees looked with some degree of contempt at the Ostjuden (Polish Jews). They were very much brainwashed with the idea that the Germans—and even the German Jews—were somehow superior, in spite of what was happening to them.

New developments started happening fast, and in spite of our experiences at the hands of our Polish compatriots, we became very patriotic, and started looking for ways to defend our country. Just before the outbreak of the war, chaos overtook the country. Radios blared patriotic slogans and songs, but no one could give any information as to where and how to volunteer for the cause. Some of my older friends went to Kielce to volunteer for the Army, only to be turned down, because nobody knew what to do. Then came the General Mobilization and all the youngsters ran to their designated mobilization centers. They later described the chaotic conditions, when in some places there were rifles and no ammunition, and vice versa.

When the war broke out on September 1, 1939, the Polish radio was claiming overwhelming victories, but it soon became obvious that things were going badly. The German Air Force was flying high over my hometown in large formations. Some of the police officers would shoot at them with rifles, even though they were 50 times higher than the range of a rifle shot.

On the third day we started seeing Polish soldiers running in disarray, retreating and shedding their uniforms and gear. Some rumors started taking over the news. One was of a big Polish victory near Kutno, where the Polish Cavalry supposedly destroyed several divisions of German infantry and tanks. The opposite, in fact, had occurred. Trying to fight tanks and armored cars with horses and sabers, the gallant Polish Cavalry was slaughtered. Fear gripped us all. Refugees from towns to the west arrived talking of mass murder of all males, but not females. Then my cousin Stefan Jutrzenka arrived from Jedrzejow. He came from a very rich family on his mother's side (Horowicz). He brought with him money, jewelry and silver in a suitcase. He talked my father into running away with him eastward, away from the advancing German Army. Stefan went out and bought a horse and buggy (which was to be gotten only at a great premium). Then he, my father, my brother, and I started our journey eastward, toward a town called Szydlow.

The road was a narrow, dusty two-lane highway made of rolled gravel. I recall that the road was very crowded with refugees, some on foot carrying their belongings, some like us on a buggy pulled by a horse. We were all civilians. There was not a single soldier to be seen. Suddenly three airplanes descended on us and started strafing. We ran off the road into potato fields and took cover. I recall that my father suddenly shook violently, and I thought that he was hit, but fortunately he was all right. To our misfortune, the horse was killed and we were left without any conveyance. Many people were injured at that time, but I don't recall seeing any dead people.

We proceeded alongside the road on foot carrying some of our belongings. As we grew tired, we started throwing away less essential items until gradually got rid of everything except the jewelry and silver. My cousin gave me some paper money wrapped in a piece of linen to carry on my waist in a belt-like fashion.

The experience of being strafed was shattering to our morale. We soon became exhausted and started doubting the wisdom of running away as a way of saving our lives. On foot, we were no match for a mechanized army. When rumors, and finally a radio news report, confirmed that the bridges across the Vistula were blown up, my father decided to turn back and go home. So, we took leave of our cousin Stefan, who decided to continue eastward. He made it across the Vistula and then into that part of Poland ove rrun by the Soviets. He survived a Siberian camp and finally joined the Polish Army in Soviet Russia before we met up with him again after the war.

I recall how people in Szydlow reacted to our arrival. They gave us food and drink and treated us very well. But this was the first time that I became aware of the lonely feeling of a refugee. The local people went to sleep in their beds, while we slept stretched out on a hard floor. To be suddenly deprived of a base and to be dependent on strangers for shelter and food—the shock was overwhelming. Although I was a very strong youngster, I did not argue with my father about his decision to return home. I was willing to take my chances at home rather than be at the mercy of strangers. And so we turned back and walked through villages along back roads, toward home.

# THE GERMANS ARRIVE

W e returned to Chmielnik just in time to witness the arrival of the German Army, in endless columns of mostly infantry and horse-drawn artillery and some columns of mechanized army. I believe it was September 5 or 6, 1939. There was no battle in or around my hometown, but there were a few casualties among the members of the militia and civilians, who were organized to hand over the town to the Germans and were shot by the first German patrols.

As I was watching the Germans, I remember saying to myself: "Look, these people are not killers as the rumors had it." They were well behaved, disciplined soldiers. Some of their officers were older men with big beer bellies, and I saw some of them saluting the older bearded Jewish men. In general, the first impression was quite favorable.

Then one night, a group of armed men went on a rampage and caught some prominent members of the Jewish community, including the Rabbis from Rakow and Checiny. The Germans locked them up in the Bet ha-Midrash (house of study), set the building on fire, and burned them alive. I believe that only two people escaped through burning windows. This was the German way of shocking the entire population and instilling a terrible fear in the community.

This was, as I later found out, the job of the special commandos (the Einsatzgruppen) of the SS force. The Germans subsequently started organizing the Judenrat, which was a tool in their hands, through which they extorted all kinds of monies and goods. Their plan was to get the most respected and trusted citizens to participate in the Judenrat so that most people would obey the orders of the Germans and mistrust the few who might resist this cooperation. They gave the Judenrat total jurisdiction over the Jewish population. Whenever money, manpower or goods were needed, the Germans would give an order to the Judenrat, and thereby obtain all they wanted without directly interacting with the people. They kept on reassuring the Judenrat that as long as they cooperated, no unusual evil would befall the civilian population. The Judenrat, in turn, believed that they would be able to somehow get around the harsh policies of the Germans through bribery or other means, and in that way gain precious time until the war's end.

I believe it must have taken a great deal of psychological study on the part of the Nazis to come up with a method that would lull the population into a kind of stupor, and then, gradually take away, inch by inch, their freedoms and erode their self-respect, ultimately forcing everybody into submission and eventually destruction.

I remember that when they started organizing the Judenrat, they sent a policeman to our house to get my father, who was not at home at the time. When he found out that they were looking for him, he went into hiding with Michuel Brikman, a candlemaker friend of his from the Mizrahi Zionist Organization. The fear of being found and punished actually destroyed my father psychologically. After that time he was afraid of his own shadow and rarely ventured out. The Germans quickly forgot all about him, but he did not forget that incident. He never recovered his self-confidence and was always afraid.

The formation of the Judenrat was followed by the formation of the Jewish Police, who were the law enforcement arm of the Judenrat. The Germans would request a labor force to clear the roads of snow, and the Jewish Police would deliver the manpower through a raid. Eventually all kinds of labor would be required and labor camps would be established, like the one in Biala Podlaska on the Russo-German demarcation line on the river Bug, to build whatever the Germans wanted.

The usual procedure was that the poorest youngsters would be sent to these camps, since the affluent people would pay a bribe to the Judenrat member, who in turn became a macher with the Gendarmerie, and bribe them to release whomever they wanted released. The Germans would brainwash the people into believing that if they held a job that was German approved, no harm would befall them. Some of the community elders wanted people to cooperate, otherwise the whole community would suffer.

Soon food stamps were introduced, and anyone caught selling food illegally would perish. Then the white armbands with a blue Star of David were introduced. Every Jew, even children and infants, had to wear one on every outergarment at all times.

The winter of 1939–1940 was actually uneventful, except that schools were closed and there were no newspapers and no radio broadcasts. Anyone caught with a radio disappeared. Rumors were circulating that the French and the British were marching into Germany, and that the war would soon be over.

The Germans annexed the western part of Poland. Then they formed the General Government of Poland with the seat in Krakow, with a German governing the remainder of German-occupied Poland.

A German paper was published in Krakow, which was available sporadically. In that paper we could not find any confirmation of the rumors of impending German defeat. But we still deluded ourselves that the war would soon be over, and therefore the most important thing was to stay alive. Thus no German edict was met with any resistance.

We started getting refugees from a town Plock, which was located in the territories annexed by Germany. These people were sent by rail, in open coal cars, with about 20 kg of luggage, which was all they were permitted to take along. They were sick and exhausted from the exposure to the cold. The Judenrat assigned them to people's homes. Food was becoming more scarce, and it was difficult to live on the food rations. The local people were able to scrounge around, mostly by risking their lives to barter some of their belongings with the farmers from the surrounding villages.

The refugees from Plock did not have anything to barter. The Jewish community formed a soup kitchen to help them out. However, gradually the help became very meager, because everybody was going hungry. Soon an epidemic of typhus descended upon the community (due to lack of soap there were lice all over), and casualties started mounting, mostly among the poorly nourished people.

At that time I joined a group formed by the Judenrat under the direction of a refugee young doctor, who was a graduate of the Medical School in Pisa, Italy, and married to a local girl, Rochma Zalcman. This group was called Komisja Sanitarna (Sanitary Commission) and was given the task of quarantining the stricken. We would carry them on makeshift stretchers through the streets to the former bathhouse, where we cared for them to the best of our ability. We were also given the job of isolating and fumigating their homes and belongings. We would close all the doors and windows and make them as airtight as possible, and then start to burn sulfur. We also boiled their clothes. Since I always wanted to become a doctor, this kind of work appealed to me, and I quickly became deeply involved.

Most of the stricken people died, but many survived. Now that I am a doctor, I do not know how we did it. Of the ten young people in the Sanitary Commission, all got sick except me. My friend Auerbach was so gravely ill that the doctor said there was no hope. His fever was 42 degrees Celsius, and he was vomiting and couldn't breathe, but somehow he pulled through only to be taken later to Treblinka.

Prior to this job I worked in a stone quarry on the road leading to Kielce and quickly became proficient in drilling with a pneumatic drill to make holes for dynamite. The smaller stones were then moved out of the quarry via hand-pushed carts, and finally they were crushed by hand with a hammer to the size of one to two inches and used for road building. I learned quickly how to strike a rock so as to get it to split easily.

The stone quarry was operated by a private German firm contracted by the German Army to build roads. We were supervised by a German Gypsy who thought that the harsher he treated us, the better off he would be. The only saving grace with this job was that I had to work only five days a week and could go home every evening for some TLC.

The summer of 1940 was a particularly devastating time. France was defeated; Belgium, Holland and Norway were occupied; and England was threatened. In spite of our distrust of German-supplied news (we even heard rumors that would deny the catastrophe in the west), we were very depressed. We would get some news from the Polish Underground, although there was nothing uplifting there. Our sources to the Underground were our friends, the Zals. Bogdan (Antoni) Zal was my brother's classmate at the gimnazjum in Busko-Zdroj. Right after the Germans occupied Poland we met Bogdan, who came to Chmielnik, and somehow we became good friends instantly. We met every so often, and eventually we came to know Bogdan's older brother, Jan, who was an aviation engineer employed by a Polish outfit in Mielec before the war. The Germans went after all the educated Poles they could find: doctors, lawyers, engineers, teachers, etc. When some of these people were found, they were arrested and never heard from again. Jan was hiding from the Germans, and he settled in a small village called Grzymala, in a partly destroyed house that belonged to his grandparents. He lived there with a woman, Mme. Zalewska, who apparently was a nurse, and had nursed Jan back to health when he was stricken with typhus in Lodz before the war. Since the Zals were farmers we would buy some food from them from time to time, which was illegal according to the German laws.

Bogdan had told me that he and Jan were members of the Armia Krajowa or AK (Polish Underground), and on another occasion he said that in view of the very difficult times, we should promise each other help when needed. We shook hands solemnly, and left it at that. Sometime later, in the winter of 1940-1941, Bogdan and a friend of his, Ziomek, came running to the ghetto, claiming that the Gestapo were on their heels. We hid them in our house, and I put a placard that was used for quarantine purposes ("Danger—Typhus") on our door. I believe Bogdan never forgot that episode.

# GRADUAL DETERIORATION
## AND THE FORMATION OF THE GHETTO

The conditions in our town deteriorated gradually. The Germans continued to extort money, jewelry, and fur. The extortions and robbery were not limited to the German government. The German merchants and entrepreneurs managed to get their share too. There was a German outfit in Oldenburg that was in the feather business. One day in the fall of 1940, they came to us with an order to open my father's warehouse, and they then emptied it of all merchandise (feathers) and trucked it away on three lorries. I can't remember the name of this firm, but it was definitely from Oldenburg, Germany. All warehouses were robbed of all available goods—leather, textiles, etc.—which were carted off to Germany. The farmers from neighboring villages had their heyday, too. They received exorbitant prices for food, paid in money, jewelry, clothing and whatever else was available for barter.

In the spring of 1941 the official formation of the ghetto was announced, and the Jews had to move from the main streets to back streets and away from the market square. Anyone caught outside the ghetto could get beaten mercilessly or killed by the Gendarmes, even though the borders of the ghetto were ill defined. Because I had to carry the sick on stretchers to the so-called hospital, I was able to move freely throughout the forbidden streets. There was no other way to get across town from one area of the ghetto to the other. On one terrifying occasion, I was crossing the market square when a Gendarme by the name of Wrede let his dog loose on me. Were it not for the intervention of a dentist, Kaufman, who apparently worked on the German's teeth, I would have been ripped apart by his dog. The dog stopped one foot away from me at the sound of his master's whistle. To this day, I cannot stand German shepherd dogs.

Even though it was a small town and the German edicts were difficult to enforce 100 percent, life was getting more and more difficult in many ways.

1. Living quarters: Between the influx of refugees and the limitations of the ghetto, every family had to satisfy itself with less living space. Some of the Polish landlords took advantage of the situation; others were helpful. In our own case, the Polish cobbler we rented from told us early in 1940 to move out and gave us very little time to do so. We then relocated to a place on Szydlowska Street that was owned by an old Polish lady, Mrs. Majowa. Her son-in-law, Mr. Zamojski, was very helpful, and he even supplied us with meat (he was a butcher) during difficult times. When the ghetto was established we had to move from the front apartment to the rear of the property. (We have pictures of it from our visit to Chmielnik in 1980).

2. Food: The allotted food coupons, enough for 600 calories per day per person, were totally inadequate to maintain one's health, and therefore we bartered everything we could for food. Mother was an excellent manager and she was always able to put together some nourishing meals. Most days we had a refugee from Plock at our dinner table. Most people, however, had extreme difficulties in feeding their families. Some people were engaged in smuggling food from outside the ghetto by bartering with the surrounding farmers. The Germans, of course, were familiar with those activities. When smugglers—many of them children and young teenagers—were caught, they were summarily executed, shot without any inquiry or trial. In addition, the Germans offered prizes to the Gentiles for capturing smugglers outside the ghetto and delivering them to the Gendarmerie. A typical prize was five kg of sugar and two liters of vodka per captive. The audacity of some of our Gentile compatriots is illustrated by the following episode: Some friends and I were standing at Magistracka Street, near our little stream, which was not far from the town line,

which Jews were not allowed to cross, when we noticed a farmer leading a Jew by a rope tied around his neck. Neither my friends nor I knew the Polish peasant, nor did we recognize the Jew, but it became very obvious that the farmer was leading him to the Gendarmerie. Without much consulting, one of my friends, Alter Miedziejewski, a very tall fellow, tripped the peasant who fell and thereby released the grip on the rope thus freeing the Jew. We all ran away and hid for several days hoping that nobody had recognized us. We were sure that the farmer would not go to the Gendarmerie and describe what happened. Fortunately we got away with it. This one minor incident is illustrative of the treatment we could expect from our Polish compatriots.

3. Clothing and Footwear: These items were at a premium. Many of our fellow Jews were making fortunes from sales of textiles and leather goods, which they managed to hide away. Whoever could afford it was able to satisfy his needs; but many people and most of the refugees were ill clad.

4. Information: News of any kind was practically non-existent. There were only rumors, and of course, German propaganda. There were some couriers from various Zionist organizations that tried to organize some kind of common action, but there were very few people who knew any details, and so more rumors circulated. Rumors had it that Mordechai Anielewicz, leader of the Warsaw Ghetto Uprising, was in Chmielnik several times as a courier.

5. Medical Care: Of course there were no hospitals, and there weren't even any doctors. Dr. Balanowski, the only Jewish physician before the war, was arrested and a Volksdeutsche physician took over his practice. People were afraid to go to him, and anyway they could not afford it. Later on, some refugee doctors were able to offer clandestine care to the very sick. Eventually Dr. Balanowski was released from prison in Busko-Zdroj, but he did not have his office any more and therefore was of little help.

6. Education: Schools were closed as soon as the Germans marched in, and they were never re-opened.

And so life went on, with everybody becoming more and more depressed and subservient to the whims of the Germans.

## YOUNG PEOPLE COPING WITH DAILY LIFE

There were daily work details doing all kinds of work, mostly road building. In the winter, life was very hard. Roads had to be kept open no matter how heavy the snowstorms, and the Germans together with the Jewish Police would close off an area and get all adults out on the road to clear the snow. Many people were poorly dressed and ill fed. During one of these lapanka (raids), we were ordered to shovel an area between two telephone poles, approximately 50 meters. Next to me was an elderly man who could not clear the snow as quickly as was required. The rigorous work made him feel ill. After I finished clearing my area, I tried to help with his section and got a terrible beating from a German soldier. He took sadistic pleasure in seeing the old man out of breath. Another time I recall being guarded by a very short fat soldier, who was a very fine person. We were shoveling during a snowstorm and couldn't make any progress because of the blowing and drifting. Our guard cursed the Nazis and told us to get some shelter. He said that if he spotted some Germans approaching, he would alert us by singing, and we could come out and start shoveling again.

In spite of all these difficulties, we never lost hope and we were actually preparing ourselves for the day when we would be free. I started taking courses in math, physics, chemistry, and biology. My teachers were university students who were stranded in Chmielnik. There was also the previously mentioned Rochma Zalcman, married to the young doctor, and another teacher who was the wife of an attorney. They were refugees from Warsaw. The young people formed a book club, and we would generally congregate in Moniek Preis's house (son of a rabbi in Montreal) to discuss various books. Sometimes we'd have a dance afterward. This is where I befriended Esther. She would teach me how to dance, and she would sing English language songs for me. The group of youngsters included natives of Chmielnik and refugees from large cities, like Warsaw, Lodz, and Krakow. Most of the non-natives were students at various gimnazjums before the war—very intelligent and exciting people. Being young and naive, it did not occur to us that we were in mortal danger. We knew that we were in for hard times, but could not have conceived of the "Final Solution."

People were trying to get jobs that were "essential" to the German war effort, believing that would keep them safe from persecution. Many young people were trying very hard to become members of the Jewish Police and were using all kinds of protekcja (influence/connections) to get nominated. Before I became a Sanitariusz, I myself toyed with the idea of becoming a policeman. Although I was very young, I was tall and very strong and had the necessary protekcja because the head of the county Judenrat was a relative by marriage—a certain Joseph Topiol, whose brother Alter Chil was married to my father's sister Esther, who lived in Palestine. Our cousins Yakov and Avram Topiol in Israel were nephews of Joseph Topiol in Busko-Zdroj, which was the county seat. Whenever Joseph Topiol came to Chmielnik, he visited with us and offered all kinds of help. However, my father refused to have anything to do with the Judenrat and their helpers, and therefore I was not allowed to become a policeman.

I remember being somewhat upset with my father's decision. Being a policeman would have prevented me from having to work in stone quarries, on the roads, etc., and eventually would have helped me avoid being sent to a labor camp in Podleze. But that was his decision. Some of the policemen were nice boys, who did the best they could and tried to help people. Others became drunk with power they thought they had and behaved miserably, taking bribes and extorting money and goods from people. Some of them acted with unnecessary force while carrying out orders. An incident that stands out in my mind happened when the Judenrat ordered the Sanitary Commission to help the policemen round up people for a labor camp. I was assigned to a certain policeman called "God's Horse," Ferleger by name. We went to Pinczowska Street to find a certain a young man from Plock. He lived in a former grain store. God's Horse went in the front entrance from the street, having ordered me to watch the window facing a courtyard, lest the young man try to escape that way. The young man did exactly that, and when God's Horse saw that I did not try to stop him, he became livid with rage and wanted to hit me. He then went to Gonczarski (his supervisor) and told him that I sabotaged the whole operation. I was arrested and put in koza (detention) overnight, but fortunately the Germans were not informed, and I was released through protekcja.

Subsequently the Sanitary Department was enlisted to round up sewing machines (toward the end of the existence of the ghetto) to create an industry that would be important to the Germans, and which would offer some security to the people employed. We were paired, one policeman to one sanitary person. I was paired with my childhood friend Hershel Maly, and we were looking with great zeal for sewing machines that some people were hiding because we were convinced that we were serving a good cause. Of course, nothing came of it anyway.

Meanwhile rumors were reaching us about wysiedlenie (resettlements) to the east, where Jews were supposedly gathered to create their own industry in a zone inhabited strictly by the Jews. Some people believed that this was true; others were very skeptical, but all of us were confused.

During that period a leader from the Zionist Revisionist Organization in town, Meir Feldman, called me and several others about forming a resistance organization. He got in touch with some Gentiles for the purpose of buying arms. Money was needed. We requested help from our elders. My father and some of his friends were ready to help, but after they contacted other elders, we were warned that we were playing with fire and that we would bring disaster to the whole town. We were told to give up such foolish ideas; otherwise we would be punished.

## ASSISTANCE FROM THE ZALS

The idea of being resettled in the east and the uncertainty of it did not sit well with me. I started exploring the idea of getting Aryan papers (false documents) that would conceal my Jewishness and enable me to be able to get away with my family. We discussed these problems with the Zals and decided to go ahead. I would have to make a trip to Tuczepy, the seat of the local government for the villages where the Zals lived, to bring money, passport pictures, etc.

On the day of the appointment, however, I got sick with a kind of gastroenteritis and bloody diarrhea, but I was the only one in the family who could get out of the ghetto. I threw away my armband, got on a bicycle, and started out on the journey to Tuczepy. I had to stop every five or ten minutes in order to move my bowels. It was a very long trip. I had to use very narrow field trails so as to avoid Poles, who could be quite dangerous. I finally arrived exhausted and weak, and the Zals took all the photos and money and went to get the papers, while I rested.

As soon as the papers were in my possession I went back home in spite of being weak and sick. Jan Zal tried to persuade me to rest a day or two, but I considered those papers so critically important for my family that I ran as fast as I could and brought the documents home on a Saturday in August 1942.

As soon as I got home I was ordered by the Judenrat to go to a labor camp in Podleze, where instead of working drying swamps and digging ditches I would be the first-aid man. I had no choice but to go.

Many people thought that this was a very good job and would offer me security, but I fortunately thought otherwise.

I was there three or four weeks. When I heard that Jews from surrounding villages were being rounded up and taken to the Chmielnik ghetto, I decided to run away. I had received a message from my father, urging me to stay in place. I would be safe in Podleze, he said. But I perceived correctly that the rounding up of the Jews from the villages was a preliminary to deportations of the Jews from Chmielnik. My friends at the camp also tried to persuade me to stay, but I was very attached to my family, and did not want to save myself, knowing that they were not safe somewhere. So, I did run away under cover of darkness.

I walked all night, then got a ride from a farmer, and finally got back home. When I sneaked into the ghetto, the first fellow who saw me was a boy by the name of Motel Strauch, who could not believe that I was so foolish as to run away from a "safe" place and come home. He then pleaded with me to give him my ausweiss (ID) from the camp, because he wanted to go there. I gave him my papers, and one week later he and all the others there were taken to Treblinka where they perished.

On Thursday, October 1, 1942, two days before I returned from Podleze, there was a roundup of all able-bodied men and women age 15-40. The Germans chased all the people into the Market Place and with the help of the Polish Blue Police and the Jewish Police, chose many men and women and sent them to Skarzysko-Kamienna, where they labored in various factories of ammunition and chemicals. Some of these people survived the war, including my father-in-law, Israel Gutman (his brother, niece, and nephews perished there). The rest of the people were let go. On that day Esther was caught and would have been sent away had our friend and member of the Jewish Police, Szymek Feingold, not intervened. He took her out of the line and sent her home. On such minor accidents did people's lives depend, and just like that they either survived or perished.

I got home on Saturday, October 3, 1942. As soon as I arrived, I got in touch with the Zals via a coded telegram ("Birthday Greetings"), which I sent through a Polish friend. We would get out as soon as the Zals responded. The day before, Sam had been taken out of the ghetto by Mme. Zalewska and Bogdan and brought to their village Grzymala, so there were three of us left, waiting to be rescued.

We were not the only ones trying to save ourselves. People would cut a deal with anybody just to escape. There were many rich and influential people who made deals with the Germans to remain in Chmielnik in the event of deportation. Many succeeded for a while. There was no concerted effort, though, on the part of the Jewish community or its leaders to do anything for the entire population. In retrospect, during my sleepless nights, I have asked myself, "What if we had refused to cooperate with the Judenrat? What if we had threatened their lives and those of the Jewish policemen—perhaps even killed a few to make our point?" They would probably have run for their lives and would not have been available to do the dirty work for the Germans. Without their help, the Germans would have had to bring a great number of people in, and their control would not have been so easily accomplished. But nothing of the sort was done, and nobody in the entire world made any effort to inform us of the terrible fate that awaited us—not the Gentiles or Jews in Poland, or Palestine, or anywhere.

On Sunday, October 4, old Mr. Zal (Bogdan and Jan's father) came by horse and wagon to retrieve us. That morning my father had been put to work unloading some trucks, but we didn't know where exactly. Thus, we were in a terrible quandary. We were supposed to leave under the cover of darkness, but father could not be located. While looking for father that morning, I visited Esther, who was my girlfriend. Although I was not sure of my feelings at the time, the sight of her made me blurt out where we were going and with whom. This was a closely guarded secret at that time. I apparently was not aware of the terrible dangers awaiting us. We were supposed to hide out for several weeks and then come back to our home, or so we believed. Esther didn't know it then, but remembering those names would later save her life.

I said good-bye to Esther with a great deal of emotion and guilt for leaving her behind, but I had no other choice. I returned home to find that my father was already there, having been released by the Germans. Mr. Zal was looking over all of our possessions and wanted to take every-thing with him. We had to plead with him that he could not possibly manage that, but he insisted that he could come back later and take every-thing with him. We also had a difficult time keeping him away from other people. This was a necessary precaution because he might have just spilled the whole story to others, putting us in danger. He was an extremely decent man, and he could not perceive the dangers facing us. Finally we found some wine and started toasting him until he got tired and fell asleep. When he awoke, it was dark. He took whatever he could fit on the wagon and made his way out of the ghetto. We headed out separately, met him on a little used side road, got into the wagon, and started on our journey. We did not even say good-bye to any of our neighbors or friends for fear that when pressed they could give us away.

Grzymala couldn't have been more than 15 kilometers away, but the journey to Grzymala was long and slow because we had to take side roads. We were very quiet, not even daring to speak. One memory that particularly stands out is how every time we went over a rock, the wagon shook, causing a mortar and pestle somewhere inside to make a disconcerting noise.

We finally got safely to Grzymala before dawn and we quickly got into the house in order not to be seen by neighbors. Sam was of course, waiting for us and so were Bogdan and Jan. They were very friendly and encouraging and tried to make our arrival very pleasant, but I immediately noticed that they asked us to whisper and not make our presence known with any noise so as not to arouse any suspicions. We were taken to an attic and spent the first night there. The next day we had a conference with Jan, Bogdan, and Mme. Zalewska and developed plans for a short stay in their house. Father had some gold coins (old Russian rubles), and he gave some to Jan to buy food with them. It was still so hard to tell what awaited us and we didn't know how far ahead to plan. My father had chronic bronchitis from heavy smoking and feather dust, and our hosts became very concerned that his cough might be heard and give us away, so he was given a pillow with which to cover his face when coughing, so as to muffle the noise.

The very next day, which was Monday, I experienced the most recriminating lesson of my life. Esther appeared at the Zals' looking for us. The Zals—especially Mme Zalewska–took it as a betrayal of a life-threatening secret. I was attacked by everybody and in essence told that if my family perished, the fault would be mine alone. They speculated that whoever took Esther to Grzymala knew where we were hiding, and therefore we were all in danger. In their conversation with Esther when she arrived, the Zals denied that we were there. They told her that we had gone to Germany as laborers and sent her away. She wandered for a couple of days, trying to hold a job as a teacher in a farmer's family, but she was finally turned out and her false papers were taken away from her. She returned to the Zals for help and eventually, after several discussions, she was taken in at my father's insistence. He promised that whatever we had for food or other necessities, Esther would share it. This deed, of course turned out to be the fundamental event in my life and the foundation of my family, for which I am so eternally grateful.

## Five in Hiding

Esther was ushered into the attic to join us, which marked the beginning of continuous harassment and criticism of me on the part of Mme Zalewska, and also to some degree on the part of my mother. I was not permitted to forget the dreadful thing of giving away the secret of our location thereby jeopardizing everybody's life.

Those circumstances caused me to resent Esther, and our relationship suffered as a result. Many times, I behaved childishly, and every time I was reminded of my own indiscretion, I took it out on Esther. At other times, though, we were friends and together dreamed of better times.

Two days later, Jan and Bogdan came in very perturbed and reported that the day before, on Tuesday, October 6, 1942, our hometown had been evacuated of all the Jews and that many Jews were subsequently found dead or dying alongside the roads. Jan told us that he was very happy to have us with him and to have spared us from such horrors. We still had no idea what to do and how to plan our future. Jan kept on reassuring us that some way out would be found for us. We discussed using our false documents to individually go to Germany as Polish laborers. There was also talk about a rumored ghetto in Sandomierz, where we might possibly settle. Anyway, the situation was very chaotic, and the best thing seemed to be to let the dust settle and then make the proper decision.

For the time being, we were lying low and not letting anyone know of our presence in the attic. And we began a saga that would go on for 22 months. We didn't know it would be so long, of course, but it seemed prudent to create some kind of emergency hiding place. We lifted some of the wood planks of the attic floor and discovered a crawl space between created by the ceiling below. We prepared a place that would fit the five of us, and after we crawled in we could then replace the planks above us, so that it looked like just another part of the attic floor.

Several weeks into our ordeal, it started to get cold in the attic, and we were moved to the pantry. Let me describe the entire place where we were hidden: It was an old farmhouse that had been inhabited by Bogdan's grandparents before they became more prosperous and moved to the large farm called Zalowka. When the grandparents died, the farmhouse was unoccupied and fell into disrepair. It initially consisted of a kitchen and a pantry on one side of the entrance hall and two small rooms on the other side of the hall. The two rooms were totally destroyed and the only habitable area was the kitchen and the pantry.

The illustration above shows the destroyed rooms that were called Pusta Chalupa (the Empty Hut). Bogdan, Jan, Mme. Zalewska, and Slawka (Jan and Bogdan's orphaned niece) lived in the kitchen. There was a staircase with a trapdoor leading to the attic from the entrance hall. Directly under the pantry there was a cellar used for storing vegetables and potatoes for the winter, also under a trapdoor. As soon as we got down to the pantry from the attic we started to build another emergency hiding place, this time in the cellar below. We fashioned a compartment of wooden boards and covered it up with potatoes. The entrance to the compartment, however, was left open. That way we could quickly get inside and then fill in the potatoes behind us. We did, in fact, spend several nights in that hiding spot.

We spent the winter of 1942-43 in the pantry. While there, I discovered a very informative listening post. My sense of hearing was very acute, and thanks to a tiny hole in a bread oven that protruded into the pantry, I was able to hear conversations held in the kitchen. Jan was the head of the Underground, and he hosted many meetings of the group in that kitchen. By listening in, I heard, to my dismay, that the AK was systematically killing Jews who were hiding in the forest and on other farms. I never heard Jan condone or agree with that practice, but neither did he vehemently disagree nor order a stop to these killings. He probably feared for his and our lives and did not want to appear overly concerned about the fate of Jews, which could arouse suspicions in other people's minds. Decent people were afraid and at times ashamed—or more accurately worried—that some of their compatriots would accuse them of being Jew-lovers. I heard through my listening post many disquieting things not concerning Jews but rather other people belonging to other political factions, specifically those of leftist leanings, who were systematically killed, as well as some of German collaborators.

Raids were also planned in that kitchen. They would stop railroad cars so that merchandise like sugar, whiskey, and other foodstuffs could be whisked away to hiding places, including the Zals' home. Our place was at times filled to capacity with sugar and other bounty. Since this was a meeting place for the Underground, we had to be ever so much more careful, and we were looking out and listening for anyone coming into the house. There were some people who, we felt, would not harm us, and others who were very dangerous. There was a young man whose mother was interned at Auschwitz, and we were not afraid when we heard him approaching, although we would not dare to be seen by him. I also remember a naval officer whom we did not fear. Then there was a fellow with the nickname Kurza Twarz ("Hen's Face"), whose approach to the house was terrifying to us. He used to play a harmonica, and every time I heard that tune after liberation I got nightmares. He was a vicious anti-Semite and regularly looked for Jews in hiding. He perished in one of the Underground in-fights.

Our lives gradually developed a pattern. Regarding washing and toilet, we were given a pail of water for drinking and washing, and another one for our toilet needs, which we covered up until the next night, when Slawka would take it out behind the barn to dispose of it at a compost dump. For food, we would get some boiled potatoes and milk for breakfast, and potatoes and scrambled eggs for dinner. Although Mr. and Mrs. Zal were delivering enough food for us all from the farm, Mme. Zalewska would not give us our share. She had a fetish about her appearance and would use milk for washing her skin. She probably never believed that we would survive, and therefore did not care about what she did or how she treated us. Meat was never served to us, but occasionally we'd find a bone in the soup, and we would chew on that bone until nothing was left on it. Esther used to say that when she became free, she would chew on bones every day of her life.

Mme. Zalewska was a curiously secretive person. While we were in the attic, we accidentally stumbled on a Jewish Bible that was hidden in the straw of the thatch of the roof. At the time, we were looking for some other way of hiding in an emergency. The book belonged to a Jewish family, the Kagans of Riga, Latvia. There was no question in my mind that the Bible belonged to Mme. Zalewska, who was a member of that family and who was hiding that fact from everybody by claiming to be a Christian.

Her little secret probably explained why she was so scared to keep us. After all, if we were discovered, somebody might think to look into her background. Every time there were rumors that the Germans might come to the village she wanted us out. One time she came in and told us that the Germans were on their way to Grzymala, and that we must leave promptly. She said that each of us should go separately, in a different direction, so as not to arouse suspicion. She made it an urgent matter of minutes, and we had no choice but to comply, and so we were leaving when suddenly Bogdan appeared and saw what was happening and aborted the whole plan. He started yelling at Mme. Zalewska: "Where are you sending them? You know they would not survive out there even one day. If the Germans didn't kill them, the Poles would!" He told us to stay under the potatoes and take our chances at remaining undiscovered. That episode prompted us to think about devising a better emergency hiding place.

Meanwhile, the late winter of 1942 brought some encouraging news from Africa, where Rommel was retreating and the Allies were landing in Morocco; and from Russia, where the German Army was retreating from Stalingrad. These events gave us hope for a quick end to the war. We envisioned all kinds of scenarios for German defeat and impending freedom for us, and these dreams and beliefs helped us survive and encouraged the Zals to keep us there.

My sense is that had the Zals known at the beginning that this situation would last 22 months, they would probably not have undertaken that burden. The gradually changing international situation and the hope that the war would end quickly were immensely important factors working in our favor.

Jan and Bogdan were very supportive and talked to us about plans for the future. Bogdan brought us books, texts from gimnazjum and liceum, and whenever our minds were not occupied with some impending disaster, we were studying. I still can't fathom how we were able to study under all that pressure. Maybe that was what saved our sanity.

Meanwhile, our expectations for a quick German defeat did not materialize, and the longer we stayed there, the worse the pressures and fears became. We could never use our regular vocal cords to speak because the house was always full of people from the Underground. In addition, the food rations given to us under Mme. Zalewska's supervision were getting smaller and smaller. Mother was particularly concerned with Sam's health. She remembered that Sam's Pott's disease was cured by good nutrition—butter, eggs, etc.—or so she was led to believe. Those items reached the house from the farm but continued to be confiscated by Mme. Zalewska. Once old Mr. Zal came to visit us and saw what we were getting for dinner. He got very upset about it, telling us that he was sending enough food for everybody. Fearful of inciting the wrath of Mme. Zalewska, we told him that this was the exception not the rule and that we were very well taken care of.

What was there to do?

We knew from peering into the house through every crack in the wall and ceiling that some of the food, specifically butter and eggs, were stored in the hallway. And so I became a thief. At night when everybody in the house was asleep I would go down the hallway and steal a small piece of butter from the pot where it was kept. I would take only one spoonful of butter and leave the pot looking just like I found it. I would also take one egg at a time for Sam, and that made mother feel much better. Although there was a small dog in the house, he knew me and never barked when he saw me take the food.

## THE BUNKER

Spring and summer of 1943 were filled with many events. The Poles were subjected to many harsh German edicts, and food was systematically extorted from farmers by a quota system, where a certain amount of food had to be delivered to the German authorities. In addition, under the pretext of not having received the required quotas, the Germans—with the help of the Polish Police—staged raids on farms and confiscated whatever they found. This problem, coupled with the fact that the Zals were prosperous farmers, gave us many sleepless nights, since we never knew when there might be a raid on our hosts.

We then started developing and finally executed a plan for a bunker that would not be easily detected. The Germans always used dogs, German shepherds who were well trained in sniffing out people. And so it was necessary to deal with that. We figured out that if the bunker were covered all around with earth, it would cover up our scent. The only outlet would have to be an air pipe. We decided that the air pipe would have to be led out far away from the house and hidden under the trunk of tree, where many dogs were leaving their scent, which could obscure ours.

Obviously, we could not dig during the day because somebody might hear us, but digging during the night in a sleepy, quiet village would also arouse suspicion. In addition, every inch of dirt dug up had to be disposed of. We had to work very quietly and very slowly, virtually spooning out the dirt and preparing one bucket at a time. Slawka and Bogdan would remove each bucket and dump it into the fields. Also, I myself, dressed like Bogdan, carried out much of the dirt in the middle of the night.

During that time, we received very encouraging news; Mussolini was deposed, and Marshall Badoglio had taken power in Italy, thus giving us hope that the war would soon be over. This gave us more of an incentive keep working to save ourselves. At the same time we heard some very disquieting news. There was a Jewish family born and raised in the Grzymala area, who lived among the farmers. They spoke like the local peasants, and in all manners behaved and resembled them. The head of that family, an old woman, was hiding among her friends for several days at a time with her 10-year-old granddaughter. One day Jan came in very perturbed and visibly shaken. He told us that this woman and the child were clubbed to death and stripped naked. He said that if anybody could do this to that woman, then he could not trust anybody in the area, and therefore we must redouble our efforts to complete our bunker. That was when we started using shovels. Somebody would stand watch outside, and whenever someone was approaching, they would give a signal to stop digging.

Our bunker was constructed as follows: We removed some wood planks from the floor and dug a trench of about 3 ½ meters long and 1¼ meters wide, and 1½ meters deep. We then installed supporting beams and covered the bunker with wood planks, which served as its ceiling, about half a meter away from the surface. Then we covered the planks with dirt to retain the floor's original appearance. We also dug through the foundation to the outside garden and put in a long pipe for air, which, as mentioned above, ended under a tree trunk.

That accomplished, we then dug a little underground pantry that was parallel to the bunker, but one meter away. Since there was no refrigeration at that time, such pantries were commonly used to store milk and dairy products. From that little pantry we dug a tunnel into our bunker, and that tunnel in turn was covered with a sliding door panel. When we wanted to enter the bunker, we would crawl into the small pantry, slide away the panel covering the tunnel, crawl through the tunnel into the bunker. Then from within we would slide the panel back into place and fill the tunnel with dirt, so as to have an air-tight area around us, save for the air pipe.

We started having drills to get into the bunker as fast as we could, ultimately only 1½ minutes. Having such a hiding place alleviated our fears to some degree. I don't know whether the place would have withstood a thorough search, but there was a raid when the Germans came in but for a short while and left after not finding anyone in the house. This was a very important and encouraging fact.

At times, when the situation got somewhat more stable and quiet we would spend some time in the attic, which was airy and spacious. I found in the attic a long, rusty knife, which apparently had been used for slaughtering pigs. In the long days of hiding I worked on that knife until it was very shiny and sharp. During those days my mind would be filled with imaginary scenarios of our being discovered and led out to our deaths. And how I wanted to cling to life! I started scheming numerous contingency plans of what to do under what circumstances. I tried to solidify my resolve not to die in vain. At least I could take one or more Germans with me when I died. I did not dare ask Jan or Bogdan for a weapon, because that would have created a whole different situation with a possibility of a fight, and, besides, I knew they would not have considered giving me a weapon. The Zals never knew of the existence of that knife.

One day in the summer of 1943, when we were in the attic and all of our hosts happened to be out of the house, German soldiers suddenly entered the house and started calling whether anyone was home. When nobody answered, they started looking around. One of them started going up the stairs leading to the attic and moved the trapdoor aside. I was standing behind a brick chimney that was close to the trapdoor with the knife in my hand. I saw first the barrel of a rifle, and then the soldier's cap. I was ready to lunge at him, when suddenly Mme. Zalewska came into the house, and the soldier began retreating down the stairs. At that moment I became drained of all strength, and almost collapsed with fear. All this in full view of my parents, Sam, and Esther. The Germans apparently were not looking for anyone in particular; they had come to requisition food from the village. The fact that I had held back for that split second, waiting for the soldier to get more into range, saved our lives.

This incident illustrates how fragile our existence was. We

were surrounded by a sea of hatred, and our lives meant very little. We subsequently heard about what happened to the son of that old Jewish lady described previously. He too was hiding in various places like his mother. One day, he was found dead on a road, murdered and stripped of his precious Polish officer's boots. His sister, Mrs. Kotlan, was also in hiding and survived. We met her after liberation, and befriended her and her little daughter, Mirka. With my big ears I also heard about a group of Jews who were hiding in the forest and were partly armed, who were disposed of by the AK.

It is very difficult in retrospect to describe my feelings, my fears, and my mistrust of everybody around me. All I know is that these happenings have warped my mind for a very long time. They are still very much in my nightmares. I feel threatened many times, and then I realize that these are imaginary threats. I believe that maybe time will continue to blunt those fears and that eventually I may be a "normal" person.

As the summer and fall of 1943 wore on, there were promising happenings all over the globe. The German offensive was halted in the east, and they were retreating. Rumors of a second front in the west were filling us with hope. Then, when the second front in the west did not materialize, it plunged us into depression, but at least the hope got us through the winter.

Then the news from the eastern front became more encouraging. The Germans could not cope with the Russian winter, and they were being beaten on a long front. We were getting all those news from the Underground press through Jan.

Meanwhile we were suddenly faced with another problem: Bogdan's sister Janina got involved with a farm hand, Kazmirek, and without the family's approval planned to marry him. During the confrontation with the family she blurted out that if the family didn't go along with her marital plans, she would denounce us to the Germans or the Underground. We had to fake an escape to Germany on false papers as Polish laborers, so as to take the heat off the Zals. Whether Janina believed it or not is still a question, but she did not denounce us to anybody, nor did her fiancé (now husband). Things calmed down somewhat, but we were never sure what the next hour would bring.

While all this was going on, we were reading and studying, and weaving plans for the future, even though we did not quite believe that there was a future for us. Mme. Zalewska never failed to persecute Esther and speak about her in the most derogatory terms. She'd say, "What is that saving herself for?" and the like. At the same time, she'd throw some barbs at me, like, "What will he ever be able to do?" She even managed to get Jan to say, while looking at my pants, which had patches all over in all the colors of the rainbow, that I would probably make a good "fordancer" (gigolo). These and other remarks surely did not help develop self-esteem and faith in my ever-so-remote future. At times, I wished that the Germans would come and finish us off. Most of the time, however, I felt that since we most likely represented only a handful of survivors (we were informed through the Underground press that most of the Jews were killed and burned in camps), we were engaged in a personal war against Hitler. We had to survive as witnesses and maybe even to perpetuate the existence of the Jewish people. If for nothing else, though, we'd survive to spite all the Jew haters, to deny them a complete victory.

Spring of 1944 brought more rumors and hopeful news. With the Germans out of Africa, and the Allies engaged in Italy, the daily and nightly barrages of German cities and factories, and finally with D-Day on the western front, our hopes were soaring high.

We had to spend many nights in the bunker because we were not sure whether Janina or anybody else would denounce us. One night, we almost finished ourselves off by accident. We foolishly tried to fry some stolen bacon on charcoal that we took with us into the bunker. We did not appreciate the fact that the oxygen was in very short supply and that charcoal was forming carbon monoxide and also using up our oxygen. We all suddenly felt ill, but we had the presence of mind to pour water on the coals and quickly open the bunker and let the air in. We were saved by a very narrow margin.

## THE RUSSIANS ARRIVE

W e were told that the Russians were progressing steadily on the eastern front, and we began listening in the dead of night for the sounds of artillery by placing our ears to the ground. Suddenly, one night in July 1944 I heard ever-so-distant tremors. From night to night the tremors became rumbles, and eventually we perceived artillery sounds.

Finally, while in the bunker in the middle of the night we heard people talking outside. The language sounded strange, but soon my parents recognized it as Russian. We dared not get out of the bunker until Bogdan gave us a signal in the morning. Then we peered through the cracks in the windows to see Russian soldiers on very emaciated horses or on foot. We did not know what to do. The Zals did not want anybody to find out that they had saved a Jewish family. The situation outside was difficult to evaluate. We could not be sure that it was safe for us to be out by ourselves, and then, where would we go? We had a thorough review and discussion of the situation with Jan and we decided to stay put for a few days and not to venture out until the situation clarified itself.

The Russians came to this village by sheer luck. They had established a bridge-head over the Vistula River near Sandomierz at the end of the summer offensive. They might have gone through or passed Grzymala, but they stopped because, unbeknownst to us, the Germans held a line about two miles away.

Bogdan became very excited about the presence of the Russians, but information was scarce because the Russians did not advise anybody of what was going on. At the same time they continued the German edict of not permitting radio receivers. Nevertheless, Bogdan went to his parents' farm, where there was ample room and grounds, and hung a wire antenna across the trees to listen to radio news with a short-wave crystal receiver that he had hidden during the German occupation. Apparently, some of Bogdan's Polish compatriots denounced him to the Russians, and he was arrested and accused of espionage and sentenced to die. While he was being held by the Russians on the farm, someone from the farm came running to us and informed us of the situation.

The Zals thought we could help because they, like the overwhelming majority of Poles and Europeans, believed the German propaganda that all Jews were sympathizers and cooperators with the Russians, if not actually in charge of the communist system. It thus made sense to them that if a Pole were arrested by a Russian communist, the only one who could intervene would be a Jew. And so Jan came to us for help. I, of course, volunteered to go to the Russians on Bogdan's behalf.

Imagine me, pale and emaciated in my rags running as fast as I could (I almost collapsed, since I was not used to such exercise) to be a rescuer. When I arrived at the farmhouse, I approached a soldier on horseback and started pleading with him in Polish about Bogdan. He obviously did not understand, but I believe that my appearance got his attention. He started inquiring in Russian what I was talking about, and who I was. An elderly Pole came to the rescue. He spoke Russian that he had learned before World War I, when that area was under Russian domination. He told the officer that I was a Yevrey, a Jew. When the officer heard the word, he became pale and got off the horse and embraced me. (This, of course, only confirmed the bystander's belief that the Jew and communist were brothers.) The officer became very emotional when I told him that my family had been saved by Bogdan and his family. He said that he would believe me when he saw my family. He commandeered a horse and a wagon and put me aboard, and we went to our hiding place, where he met my family. He hugged and kissed everybody and told us that he was a Russian Jew from Kuybishev. And that was how we met Capt. Schneidklotz.

We entreated our new friend to wait until the evening to take us out of our hiding place to minimize the number of Poles who would find out that the Zals had saved Jews. How ironic it was that we found ourselves trying to help the Zals cover up their humane behavior, which would likely result in a hostile reaction on the part of their neighbors. (In fact, years later when we wanted to register the Zals as Righteous Gentiles in the Yad Vashem, they pleaded with us by mail not to. It was many more years later, after Jan had already died of a heart attack, before the anti-Jewish climate changed in Poland, and we were able to confer those honors on the rest of the family.)

Capt. Schneidklotz immediately ordered the release of Bogdan and took charge of us and our safety. He requisitioned a room in a farmhouse, with real beds and chairs, and placed a sentry in front of our door to protect us from the Poles, whom he did not trust. He brought food and also a radio and told us to listen only to Radio Moscow. He told us that we would likely be visited by another officer, who was also Jewish, by the name of David, though he advised us not to discuss politics with him, because he was a Party man. We followed his advice. When David came to visit us we had only praise for their system. David spoke fluent Yiddish, unlike Capt. Schneidklotz who did not even understand it. Another wonderful Russian was Capt. Bykov, a non-Jew, who came to us and helped us a great deal with his warmth and friendship.

After several days it became apparent from our talks with the captain that the Germans were still close by. One day the Germans started a counterattack and we witnessed a real battle. The Germans were heading out of the forest with tanks, and the Russians were dug in with machine guns and anti-tank weapons. I can still see today the whole thing: The German tanks were coming and the Russians were playing an accordion. When the tanks finally came close enough, the Russians opened fire. The artillery from behind us helped with several salvos, and the Germans turned around and retreated. Shooting continued, though, and the captain decided to get us out of there and send us across the Vistula to the eastern part of Poland.

Traveling by wagon and accompanied by Capt. Bykov, we journeyed eastward. We encountered columns of lightly wounded Russian soldiers marching in our direction away from the front line. They were extremely kind to us. Some of the soldiers were Jewish, and when they found out who we were, they insisted on our taking gifts from them. One young boy took out from his backpack a pair of ladies' shoes, which he was apparently carrying home for his girlfriend or sister, and he insisted that Esther take them. They were too small, though.

When we arrived at the Vistula, we had to wait a long time to cross on the pontoon bridge, which was the only way to go, as the main bridge had been blown up by artillery fire. As soon as we got across we found ourselves in the midst of a Russian outfit. A young officer came by and realized that we were survivor Jews. He started crying and hugging my mother, repeating over and over again: "U mnie tozhe takaya matushka!" (I also have such a momma!) He kissed her so hard that he loosened one of her front teeth.

It was in that area on the eastern bank of the Vistula that we met some other Jewish survivors and joined up with them as we walked further eastward. As we passed Polish villages, peasants gawked at us along the roadside. We never encountered a single person with a friendly greeting or an offer of food or water. Instead, many of them would yell out: "Look, the Jews are coming out like mushrooms after a rain!" There was no compassion for our suffering, just more hatred, belligerence, hostility, and contempt.

Theirs was not the only hatred we encountered. While the Russian soldiers were extremely friendly and helpful, their political outfits were not. One day on the road, we were suddenly surrounded by a group of men whose uniforms were different from those of the regular Russian army. We were taken to a farm and told to sit on the grass. Then I was picked out from the crowd of 12 or 13 people. They took me inside and subjected me to a frightening interrogation. I was accused of being a German shpion (spy) and a German plant, because no Jew survived the war unless he cooperated with the Germans and was still serving the German cause against the Russian people. All Jews were killed except those who cooperated with the Germans, they insisted. They went so far as to shoot a revolver behind my head to scare me into confessing. The people outside heard the shot and thought for sure I was dead.

During that interrogation, many anti-Semitic invectives were hurled at me. I became very incensed and upset and started screaming that they may as well kill me because they would never get away with this kind of treatment. Justice would prevail, I insisted, and they would be punished, since I believed in Soviet justice. Of course, in retrospect this was a childish outburst, but somehow an officer walked in and started reprimanding the interrogator (whether he meant it or not, I will never know), and he told me that we should leave as soon as possible. We then continued our trek to a town called Lezajsk.

When we got to Lezajsk we met several Jewish survivors, among them a young boy by the name of Brody, who took us to his late parents' house. He took in all the Jewish people he could find, some of them natives of Lezajsk, others like us from different areas. Before we even had time to rest from our travels, we discovered threats painted on the walls and window shutters: "Jew bastards get out of our town or we will kill you!" We were very upset and frightened, but Mr. Brody was not very concerned with these threats. He claimed the townspeople would not dare do anything to us. He went to the local militia and reported the threats, but I do not recall what they told him.

I took those threats seriously, though, and was very uncomfortable with our situation. Knowing what the Poles were capable of, I decided to get out of that place. There were 12 of us in the house, and I discussed it with the whole group and suggested that we all go to a larger city together, namely Lublin, which was the seat of the Provisional Polish Government. I was not successful in persuading everybody to leave, but my parents agreed to go, along with Mrs. Kotlan and her daughter. We went to the railroad station and boarded a freight train loaded with crates of war materiel—bombs, shells, etc. We sat on top of the crates and arrived in Lublin safely.

Unfortunately, my fears about Lezajsk were justified. Several days after our departure, hand grenades were thrown into the house sheltering the Jews. A pregnant woman was killed, and Mr. Brody lost a leg. (He now lives in the U.S. and has a car franchise somewhere on the North Shore of Long Island.)

# *LUBLIN*

We arrived in Lublin very poorly dressed and without shoes. Fortunately it was mid-summer and quite warm. We made sandals out of braided straw with cloth strips across the foot. We had no money and no food. We were told to go to a place where a Jewish philanthropic organization was helping people like us. I stood in line for a long time, and when I finally got in, I was confronted by a very fat person who started interrogating me, trying to find out whether I was in fact Jewish. He gave me a very hard time asking all kinds of questions, which got me very upset, and with tears in my eyes I picked myself up and left. Whether he was an American or not, I don't know. He called me back and I refused to talk to him. (Now, of course, I understand why I was interrogated so carefully. Many SS men were trying to pose as Jews.)

This confrontation served me very well, because right then and there I decided that I would rather starve then be robbed of my dignity by requesting some food. I went outside that building and noticed various advertisements on the wall—people looking for members of their families and friends. Among those plastered paper bulletins I found one seeking a person to chop wood for a baker. I ran there as quickly as I could, and when the baker heard what I came for, he told me that that job was already taken. However, when he noticed how upset I was with the news, he told me to chop wood for the next few days. For that work, I was given a very large, round, crusty 2 kg (4½ lb) loaf of bread, with which I ran to my family. They had rounded up some tomatoes, and we had a feast, the taste of which still lingers in my gustatory memory. Subsequent to that episode, I did everything I could in order not to have to stand in line for bread. (I still cannot stand in line for food, or even to wait at a restaurant more than several minutes before being seated.)

We found shelter in a large building called Dom Pereca (The House of Peretz), named for a well-known Jewish writer. It was supposed to have been made into a Jewish school, but the war interrupted the construction. Thus, the interior was unfinished. But it served as a shelter for refugees. In that house we, as a family, took a job as janitors. It was our responsibility to clean the floors and toilets. Polish toilets, unlike any others that I have seen, were usually piled up with feces. People did not sit on the toilet seat; instead they squatted on the top of the seat and most of the time they missed the hole causing a pile-up.

Nevertheless, we were happy to do the job and to be able to earn our keep. After a short while, we moved to a small basement, where Father built a cooking stove out of bricks (which were plentiful in the heaps of rubble from bombed out buildings) and mortar, and mother began cooking soups and other foods and selling them. That enabled us to give up our janitorial job.

Then I got a job that required me to go through the German storage facilities, which contained items robbed from the Jews before they were killed in the Majdanek extermination camp. Among items I found was a small Torah, which I gave to my cousin Moshe Ben Shachar to take to Israel for display at the Museum. (I never found out what he did with that Sefer Torah.) I also brought home a prayer book, which we still have at home, as well as a silver Atarah or diadem from a talith, and a small, silver Star of David.

Several days later, the Russians captured five Germans who had been top officers at the Majdanek camp. When they were led through the streets toward the court house, surrounded by a wall of Militia members, many people—including me—tried to get to them to beat them up. But we couldn't reach the Germans, and instead many people were hurt in the crush of the mob. The Germans were convicted of crimes against humanity and sentenced to death by hanging. I watched their execution. They were standing on the back of five trucks under the gallows, and then the trucks moved out from underneath them, causing them to strangle. It was a gruesome sight, but one worth witnessing.

Soon thereafter we were able to help other people on a limited scale. We were very fortunate to have an intact family, which at that time was very rare. Most people, with the exception of the returnees from the Soviet Union, were single orphaned survivors.

Esther was always on the lookout for "special cases," and she would bring them home, where we tried to help them individually as much as we could. One such needy person who stands out in my memory was a young boy in rags. He was about 12 or 13 years of age, but he acted tough, trying to prove how independent he was. He dreamed only of having cash to buy a supply of cigarettes, which he could sell at the train station, etc. He rigged up a chest high held tray for this purpose. We bought him some shoes and pants. Many years later, while traveling in Manhattan on the Lexington subway, I was grabbed and hugged by a strapping young man. I did not recognize our former special case (young children grow up). He was working in a radio electronic store. He insisted that I come to the store one day and he would try to repay me for what we did for him in Lublin. I reacted very immaturely, since we were brought up in the spirit of "Tzedaka," that charity should definitely go unrewarded, and I refused. In my great rush to arrive at the hospital on time, I did not get his phone number, which I regret, since it would have been nice to see him settled.

We were now living in large attic room, which served as a gathering place as well as a hotel for whomever we found. First we found a distant cousin by the name of Cukierman, who survived the war in Siberia. He was an old bachelor with many peculiarities. He slept on the floor on a straw-filled mattress.

The next relative we found was my first cousin Wolf Wygnanski, who escaped from Skarzysko-Kamienna labor camp. He also stayed with us in the same single room sleeping on the floor.

At that time I wanted to send message to our relatives in Palestine and the U.S. that we were alive. What better place to go to than the Ministry of Communication of the Provisional Polish Government under Wanda Wasilewska? When I arrived at the Ministry, however, I could not communicate with anybody, since they all spoke Russian and not Polish. Of course, no message was sent until much later when some Polish people were hired.

The next relative we found was a cousin, Moshe Jutrzenka, whom we noticed on the street while walking with Esther. He was elegantly dressed, carrying a briefcase-satchel, in the company of a uniformed person. He made it known to us in body language not to approach him but to wait for him. He then came to us after he parted from his companion. We hugged and were very happy to meet. It became obvious that he was not admitting to being a Jew and did not want to be exposed. He came with us to our apartment and sized us up. He then opened his satchel, which was filled with bank notes, and told us to help ourselves to whatever we needed. By that time, though, we were already established and proud. We thanked him but did not take anything. He survived the war with the help of a Christian woman who had fallen in love with him and had protected him throughout the war. He married that lady and emigrated to Montreal, where he died about 15 years ago from a heart attack.

We then met up with a young girl by the name of Jadzia, whom Esther brought to our home. She survived in horrifying circumstances. She was from Warsaw and was the daughter of the co-owner of street transportation in the ghetto. She was married to a ghetto policeman and remained in the ghetto almost to the last transport out to Treblinka. Due to appropriate influence she remained in Treblinka until the final liquidation of the camp, when all detainees were shot at the edge of ditches, including her parents and her husband. She was shot in the thigh and lay for hours beneath the bodies. At night, she crawled out of the ditch into a nearby forest and hid there. Then next morning, a peasant woman found her, brought her food, and helped her survive until the Soviets came. She subsequently married Romek and settled in Haifa, Israel.

Soon thereafter a medical school named for Marie Curie Sklodowska opened in Lublin. Since there were many applicants, it was necessary to take an admissions examination. I took that examination, passed it, and was admitted.

Several weeks after I began at the medical school, the Polytechnic Institute opened in Lublin and Sam got in and started his studies. I don't think that his experiences in that school were as bad as mine. He did extremely well and soon became the top student.

Bogdan also came to Lublin and applied for the examination to medical school with me. Unfortunately he did not pass the examination and was heartbroken. Seeing his disappointment and suffering, I came upon an idea to help him out. At the time, a school of veterinary medicine was also opening. I knew that the dean of the school was Prof. Parness. The name sounded Jewish, and my thought was that maybe I could convince this man to let Bogdan enter the veterinary school and take the basic studies, possibly transferring to medical school later. I requested an appointment with Prof. Parness and told him all about what Bogdan did for us and what a valuable human being he was, who would make a contribution to Poland if given a chance. He listened attentively and asked why I came to him with that story. I answered that I had the feeling that he would understand why I felt so strongly about Bogdan. He kept on looking at me, and finally I saw that he was moved. He asked me to send Bogdan to him. And that was how Bogdan was admitted to the veterinary school. He never bothered to switch to medical school and became a prominent veterinarian in charge of veterinarian medicine in the whole Szczecin region of Poland.

I gave up all my business connections and started studying with great zeal. I was the only officially known Jew in the class. There were at least four more students whom I knew to be Jewish, who were keeping their identity under wraps. One girl, who called herself Izabella Malinowska, was hard to figure. I was almost positive when I met her that she was not Jewish, and yet she was persistently friendly to me. Eventually, Izabella introduced me to her parents, who did not hide as non-Jews.

The anti-Semitism of most of my fellow students was palpable and very painful. I became one of the top students, if not the top student, which brought out envy and hatred. It got to the point where I could not tolerate the remarks made behind my back but within earshot. One time, I was walking out of class with Maya, a Jewish student who had recently arrived from England with her parents, when I could not help but hear the terribly anti-Semitic remarks made behind me. I turned around and spotted one student who looked defiantly at me. I asked him to repeat what he had said, and he looked me straight in the eye, as if daring me to do anything about it. Not willing to take any more insults to Jews, I stepped over to him and punched him on the chin with such force that he stumbled down half a flight of stairs. I then asked if anybody else had something to settle with me. Nobody volunteered.

Of course, that incident created a major uproar in school, and I was summoned to the office of Prof. Raabe, the rector of the university. He gave me a lecture about the unsuitability of using force at an institute of higher learning, etc. I, in turn informed him of my determination not to let anybody insult my people and reminded him of the behavior of Polish students before the war—how they used to throw Jewish students at the University of Warsaw, Krakow, Lwow, and others out the windows after beating them up. He stood there flabbergasted for a while, unable to say anything, until he finally stretched out his hand and said: "As the rector of this university, I have to reprimand your act. But as a human being, let me shake your hand." That was that, and I felt good. Prof. Raabe subsequently became the Polish ambassador to Moscow, I was told.

The funny thing was that the Polish students would come over to me in he library and ask me to explain certain problems, like I was just another student. But I was never invited to any of their homes. The student whom I had punched had the audacity to come to me several months later to ask me to help him. Apparently his father had been arrested by the Russians, and he wanted me to intervene. This illustrates the stupidity on the one hand, and the audacity on the other, of some Poles. He probably believed that because I was Jewish I could just call up Stalin or his secretary and secure help for his father. By the same token, he was not embarrassed to ask me for help. I told him that if I had all the power in the world, which I did not have, I certainly would not go out of my way to help him.

There were similar but less important skirmishes with my fellow students, and the end result was apparently a plan to kill me. Izabella's boyfriend, Michal, who was an army officer, had friends in the Security Service. They apparently told him of a planned attack. He and some of his friends set a trap for the would-be assassins, but nothing materialized. It is possible that word of the trap got out.

That was a how a survivor Jew existed and functioned at an institution of higher learning. I was never involved in politics in post-war Poland, nor did I have friends who were. It was not because of my politics but because of my professed Jewishness that I was hated.

# LODZ AND CHMIELNIK REVISITED

Sometime in January 1945, the Russians resumed their offensive against the Germans and pushed across the Vistula River, freeing Lodz, as well as my hometown, Chmielnik. My father, Esther, and I set out to see who had survived and gather information about our families. Of course, there was no public transportation, so we hitchhiked on the roads, getting lifts from the Soviet soldiers. They were very kind to us, inviting us aboard their open trucks, and sharing with us their food rations whenever we stopped on the road for a meal.

We arrived in Chmielnik and had to wrap our minds around the fact that mass murder was actually carried out. There were only a handful of survivors. I could not find any of my friends or family, nor could I get any information. The Polish inhabitants greeted us with hostility, particularly because they suspected that we carried some kind of authority at the behest of the Soviets. We quickly turned back toward Lublin.

Meanwhile, as Lodz was liberated, Esther decided to go on a similar fact-finding mission there. After she went to Lodz, Bogdan and I moved in together in a place on Grodzka Street and tried to feed ourselves as best we could. Both of us were crippled by our upbringing in terms of being able to prepare any food. There were no restaurants, nor any university cafeterias. The only thing we could do was to go to the market every day and buy a piece of liver, an onion, and a bit of lard, and fry it up in a pan. That, with bread and potatoes, was our daily dinner. But we survived and did well in school.

Then Jan and Slawka came to Lublin and moved in with us. Because of the threat against my life—and possibly just plain old paranoia—I felt insecure there and moved out. Izabella and Michal shared a large apartment conveniently close to the university, and they let me live there with them for the rest of the academic year.

This incident illustrates the insecurity and paranoia that possessed me: One day I left for the university very early. Izabella, who arrived later, told me that a Russian had come by the apartment looking for me. Since many people used to disappear when visited by Russians, I was afraid to remain in class and also afraid to go home for fear of being arrested. Many people were sent away to Siberia, many of them arrested mistakenly, since they had nothing to do with politics. But once you were taken away, there was no way to appeal your conviction or sentence. The Russian turned out to be Dr. "Pulkovnik," a colonel in charge of a field hospital, who wanted to meet me because he was Jewish and found out that I was the only Jewish medical student at the university. We met, and he was the kindest and warmest man. He'd lost his family in Kiev and wanted to help me and give me all kinds of things, which I, of course declined. We exchanged a great deal of information regarding Jewish persecution, and finally he asked me whether I could get him in touch with the Jewish Underground, which was smuggling survivors out of Poland to Palestine. I had some knowledge of whom to contact, but in spite of his apparent warmth and straightforwardness, I was afraid that he might represent a cover for the NKVD. I trusted no one.

I did well on my final examinations, and Prof. Stelmasiak invited me to become a part of the Anatomy Department for the next academic year. Most of the professors and many intellectuals had been killed, and there was a tremendous scarcity of teachers in Poland.

In the meantime, I went to Lodz to join the family, who in the interim had found a place to live on the Avenue of the 11th of November. The apartment needed furniture. We went to the city authorities and were sent to a warehouse loaded with furniture confiscated from the Jewish inhabitants of Lodz during the German occupation. Esther had meanwhile found a friend from before the war, Lutek, who was a member of the Polish Militia. Lutek helped us obtain a horse and wagon to bring the furniture from the warehouse to our apartment. Four Volksdeutsche (ethnic Germans) who supposedly collaborated with the Nazi regime were assigned to carry and load the furniture for us. They were supervised by a militiaman, who kept on hitting them at every opportunity, making their lives miserable. He urged me to do the same, but I could not hit grown men whom I did not know. The militiaman then accused me of being a German lover. Those are the breaks.

As it turned out, the next day a German maid who worked for Izabella's parents, who also moved to Lodz, told them that her father, a dentist, had committed suicide after being beaten while loading furniture. I was very relieved that I did not touch those men.

Meanwhile my parents had started doing business buying textiles and selling them at the market place from a stall. I joined them and became familiar with various qualities of textiles. Not long after that, Esther's father, who survived five concentration camps, found out through the grapevine that his daughter had survived and lived with us. He came to stay with us, as described by Esther.

The situation in Poland became very tense with the Russian occupation and the Polish Communist government, and we continued to suffer for being Jewish. One time Jan brought his good friend Mr. Levinsky to visit from Tuczepy, a neighboring village. He was the elementary school principal there. Jan, Sam, and I were reminiscing about the difficulties we'd experienced in Grzymala. He told us he had known we were hiding in the Zals' home, which I doubted was true. He then announced that he felt he should be rewarded for the simple fact that he did not disclose our presence. I told him I felt embarrassed that he would ask to be rewarded simply for behaving decently, without any effort on his part. Since the Russians were there, and we were free, his request did not evoke any fear.

Gradually, we were becoming convinced that we had no future in Poland and that the best thing to do might be to get out while the borders were fluid. It took a crisis, though, to really get us moving. One day a band of three assassins arrived at our home with very evil intentions. We had given a room in our apartment to a woman from Chmielnik, Hinda Kleiman, who had survived with her husband. Mrs. Kleiman's cousin happened to be visiting on the day the assassins came. When the doorbell rang, the cousin answered it and was immediately shot. I was in the bathroom when I heard the bell and then the shot in the apartment. I quickly pulled up my pants and looked out the bathroom door. I could see my father, my mother, and Mrs. Kleiman standing with their hands up in the air, and a man with a gun pointed at them. (The other two gunmen apparently were in the other room holding Mrs. Kleiman's husband and the wounded cousin.) Without much thinking, I jumped the gunman and grabbed the muzzle of the gun, while he was holding the grip. We struggled quietly for a few seconds while my father was frozen with fear, still holding his hands up in the air. I managed to trip the man, and then he was on the floor together with me holding on to the muzzle. Father finally picked up a very heavy oak chair and hit him on the head, which made the man loosen his grip on the gun. Now that I had the gun, I tried to shoot him but to no avail. There was apparently a malfunction in the gun, and there was no bullet in the chamber. Meanwhile the other two gunmen came running, but when they saw me—I was stylishly dressed, wearing Polish officers' polished boots and jodhpurs with a short Eisenhower jacket, looking almost like a military man—with a gun in my hand, they turned tail and climbed out through the window along the drainpipe (one flight down) and escaped.

Unable to shoot the remaining assailant, I beat him unconscious and left him on the floor. Not knowing whether there were more bandits in the house, we escaped through the back door and up the stairs to the attic of the building. Meanwhile, Esther had alerted the police at the precinct across the street. When they arrived, we came down from the attic and surrendered the gun to the police. On the floor we found the magazine and bullets that fell out of the gun when I was struggling with the gunman. It was actually quite fortunate that the magazine had failed to engage the next bullet into the chamber. Had I shot the bandit, I would have never been able to leave Poland.

We gave a deposition to the police but we were not in Poland during the trial. The cousin who was shot was initially paralyzed. After surgery to remove the bullet and more than a year of therapy, however, he was able to walk again. The bullet removed from his spine was matched to the gun taken away from the captured assassin, who was convicted and hanged.

# OUT OF POLAND

Following that experience, we could think of nothing but escaping from Poland—but to where? After the defeat of Nazi Germany, we initially believed that the civilized world would try to right the wrong done to us. Instead anti-Semitism in Russia and Poland was at its height. The Russians would, for instance stop a Russian Jew amputee from the war and ask him: "Hey, Abrasha, gdie ty nuzhku potiral, v Tashkentie?" (Hey, Abie, where did you loose your leg, in Tashkent?) Tashkent, a city in Central Asia, was the center of black marketeering and a place where all evacuees from Central Russia and Moscow were sent during the German advances. The insinuation was that the Jews did not fight, and if anyone of us lost a leg it was not while fighting the Germans. This in spite of the fact that the Soviet government's data clearly indicated that the Jews as an ethnic group had the highest percentage of decorated soldiers. As for the Poles I have already given plenty of examples of how they behaved.

As for other countries, Britain slapped an embargo on Palestine and searched every ship for escaping refugees, turning them back to Europe or to internment camps in Cyprus. As far as the U.S. was concerned, there was the McCurran Walter act proscribing entrance of refugees from Europe, except for a small number of quotas for people who had guaranteed jobs and other resources.

In short, we were in a quandary, not knowing what to expect but knowing that we had to get out of Poland. Our plans solidified when our previously described cousin, Stefan Jutrzenka, with whom we ran from

Chmielnik at the start of the war, surfaced suddenly after surviving in a Russian Gulag. He had become an officer in the Polish army that was formed at that time in the Soviet Union. He wanted to get out of Poland as much as we did, and so he proposed that we simply board a train for Berlin with permits to be obtained by bribes. He had heard that most people going west to Germany were not questioned, and that uniformed officers almost never were. So, we sold all our possessions and textile merchandise, bought Allied Occupation currency on the black market, and embarked on our escape trip. Once in Berlin, we planned to go from the Russian Zone to the American Zone in the southern part of Germany and get help from Jewish organizations. Rumors had it that from Germany there were many escape routes from Europe. Nobody really had any hard data, and since I did not trust anybody I was very skeptical about possible help from anybody.

On December 16, 1945, we boarded a train in Poznan in two groups: Esther, Sam, and me in one compartment, and Father, Mother, Esther's father, and Stefan in another. As luck would have it, the border guard was in the same company as Stefan, and he saluted when he saw him, and that was it. Sam, Esther, and I, however, were taken off the train by the border police. Before we were interrogated we managed to get rid of the Allied currency, the possession of which was illegal. (We dumped it in into a pile of snow.) First we were searched. One of the border guards, the apparent leader, took a beautiful Tissot pocket watch out of my pocket. Then he told us that trying to cross the border illegally carried the penalty of a labor camp in Siberia. We were very frightened. At that moment I resorted to a tremendous gamble (which could have cost me my life), but I was young, careless, and impulsive. I told the guard that in that case we would probably be neighbors in Siberia, since I knew that Soviet officers had no right to search and confiscate personal property for themselves and that everybody saw him take out a watch from my pocket and put it into his own. He got red-faced and very angry, took the watch from his pocket and threw it on the table. I reacted by telling him that this would not help, since many more people saw that he took the watch from his pocket and threw it on the table. I also told him that I saw the number on his cap. He looked at us and angrily shouted to get out of his sight, or he would do something terrible. I still don't know to this day why he didn't shoot us as we ran away. Audacity had paid off again.

We quickly left the border station. Another Russian soldier told us that in exchange for some token (I don't remember what) he would advise us how to get over the border. He accepted Sam's cheaper watch and gave us directions heading parallel to the rail line. We walked into an East German rail station, where we took a local train loaded with people (some rode on the roofs) to Berlin. We got into the car because we spoke Polish, a language similar to Russian, and the German populace was very intimidated by the Russian occupation forces—and actually afraid of us.

Fortunately, we had pre-arranged a meeting place in Berlin, in the event that any of us became separated from the group. We would meet at an address known to my cousin Wolf Wygnanski, who had some dealings with the people there. When the three of us arrived in Berlin it was late and almost dark. As we emerged from the train station, we met an elderly lady who looked at us with curiosity and approached us asking whether we were Jews. When we replied in the affirmative, she hugged and kissed us and insisted that we go home with her that night. That was how we met Tante Rosa, a Jewish lady who survived the war in Berlin with the help of her German friends. She sent a messenger to the prearranged address to let our parents know that we were all right, and the next day he brought them to Tante Rosa's house. We stayed with her for ten days.

From there we crossed to the American Zone of Berlin. We found there a Jewish organization that was helping refugees. I made an appointment with an American rabbi, and when I was ushered into his office I saw a uniformed bare-headed, clean-shaven officer with his feet on the desk. He didn't look like any rabbi I'd ever seen, and I started backing out, excusing myself in broken German for coming into the wrong office. He started laughing. This was apparently not the first time someone reacted to his appearance this way. He explained that he was an army officer, a Chaplain. He was very friendly and helpful. He had us read from a Hebrew prayer book to make sure we were Jews. He arranged for us to be taken out of Berlin in an American army truck to the British Zone in Germany. (Berlin itself was surrounded by the Russian armed forces.)

On the truck, we encountered our first black soldier. He was the driver, and he was very nice to us. He took us to Kassel railroad station, which was mobbed with refugees, German and others, where some Catholic nuns gave us soup and bread. It was delicious. There was no food to be bought.

From Kassel we took a train to Munich and stayed in the Museum, where all refugees were housed temporarily. From there we were taken by truck to a Displaced Persons camp in Landsberg. (This was the same Landsberg where the imprisoned Hitler wrote his Mein Kampf.) The day we arrived in Landsberg I saw a man from Chmielnik, Szyja Biedra, who was a collaborator with the Germans and particularly vicious. When I advised the DP camp authorities about this man, I was told that there were no applicable laws for punishing him. This was very shocking and upsetting to me, as were many other things, including influence peddling in order to get anything accomplished.

We soon discovered that my predisposition not to trust anybody was valid. There was no place to go except to stay in a DP camp in Germany. Nobody offered any hope to get out of there to be able to plan for a new life. The world powers were stuck with us and probably annoyed that we survived, thus creating a problem for them. Nor did we find that our relatives abroad were particularly eager to come to our assistance. To the contrary, we received a letter from Aunt Helcia in Palestine asking us to send her a piano from Germany to assist her daughter's education.

# *A STAY AT NEU FREIMANN*

We were moved to another DP camp near Munich called Neu Freimann, which was a great improvement in terms of living conditions. We were given a little Cape Cod type house consisting of four rooms and a kitchen, where my parents, Sam, Esther, and I, as well as Esther's father and Cousin Stefan lived. The camps had a fence and a gate where everybody had to stop coming or leaving. We were given meager food rations, and as it turned out, we were being robbed by a Jewish American former army officer named Sol Wachtel, who was the camp commander. He was selling on the black market many articles of food, etc. that were allocated to us by the UNRRA and supplemented by the AJDC (American Joint Distribution Committee).

The most galling thing about this man was the fact that he continuously kept threatening the inhabitants of the camp that if he caught anyone engaging in black marketeering he would place these people on a black list that would forever eliminate them from possible emigration to the U.S. At one meeting with the camp residents, he spoke from a balcony and was particularly nasty, at which time I, with my usual temper, protested loudly that things in the camp are not very "kosher" and an inquiry might be helpful. He then invited me to his office. He kept heaping praise on me, saying that he respected people who were studying and trying to improve themselves. He was trying to appease me with promises of extra rations of food as a reward for going to school. Of course, I refused. We had enough food since Esther worked and was able to supplement our rations with purchases at the American PX store. However, after our encounter I think that he increased the rations somewhat for all the camp inhabitants. From my point of view he and the likes of him had the same mentality as the Capos in the concentration camps (get whatever you can as quickly as possible at whatever price for yourself).

Hy Wachtel was later replaced by a most wonderful, honest, compassionate human being. Our new camp commander was Sol Sorrin from the Bronx, who helped whomever and whenever he could. He would talk to the refugees as his equals without condescension.

We finally settled in and worked and studied very hard. We had to get up about 5 a.m., so as to be able to get to the tram before 7 a.m., and to school at 8 a.m. We walked most of the time from Neu Freimann to Parzival Platz, a distance of about 2 km. That walk was particularly difficult in the winter cold. The "Amis" (what the Germans called the Americans) would not give us a lift when we tried to hitchhike.

The first day at the University of Munich was an eye opener. We were seated in our amphitheater/lecture hall, and my German fellow students on either side of me were busily writing down, in shorthand, every word the professor uttered, including, as I found out later, the jokes he made. I, on the other hand was busy trying to understand what the lecturer was saying. German medical terms were new to me. It was very disheartening and depressing. The next day the German students had all the notes neatly transcribed and typewritten, and again they were busily noting everything in shorthand. I was very disturbed by it and jealous of their robotic abilities. For a while I did not believe I could keep up with them, but eventually it turned out that listening to the professor and understanding what he said was more important in the long run, as my grades showed. I settled in, studied hard, and did very well.

At the University I did not encounter any particular anti-Semitism from my fellow students. At the same time, though, I did not form any friendships with the German students, due to my avoidance of any contact with them. I must admit that they behaved in a more civilized fashion than my fellow citizens-students in Poland. There were some incidents when docents would pointedly grill me very hard on exams, trying to trip me sometimes successfully, other times not. During my final examination in obstetrics I was to deliver a baby. The docent of course, had assigned me to a woman who was a paraplegic following an injury to her spine. When I did a rectal exam to determine the presenting part, I was stymied and could not figure out what I felt. When I informed the docent about my problem, he was obviously delighted and had that hateful smirk that I knew so well on his "Schmitze" scarred face. He examined the patient and did not say anything to me but walked out. He returned after a few minutes with the chairman of the department, Prof. Redwitz, who asked what the problem was. I candidly explained that I could not identify the presenting part and gave him a complete history and summary of findings.

He then examined the patient and asked the docent what his opinion was. The docent gave him double talk. The professor then asked me for my examination sheet, which we always had with us, and quickly wrote down "Ausgezeichnet!" (Outstanding). When he saw the surprise on my face, he said that being able to admit that one does not know is more important than to know. This was a very important message for me and had a lasting impression throughout my medical career. It turned out that the baby was born anacephalic and was left to die shortly after.

While at the university, I became involved with the Jewish Students Union and was for a while in charge of cultural activites at the Union. The Students Union was able to arrange for a plan by which students were able to get a hot soup dinner. I had a family and always had food on the table, but most of my fellow students were less fortunate. For them, a plate of hot soup and some other food was life saving.

One of the most disturbing events that I remember was when at a students meeting in the winter of 1947–1948, it was decided that we would volunteer to go to Palestine to fight for the Jewish State. I was elected among others to go to the representatives from the Jewish Agency to elicit a promise that whoever survived the conflict would be able to finish his studies in Israel-Palestine.

We met with a representative at Mehl Strasse. I believe his name was Dr. Friedman. He declared that the Jews in Palestine need chalutzim (farm workers-pioneers), and not scientists, doctors, engineers, dentists, etc. I tried to explain to him how senseless this policy was, as a new state would need all kinds of experts. It was to no avail. He was not to be convinced and he refused our request to get in touch with his superiors to ask for their opinion. He declared that he was well aware of the policies of his superiors. After some sharp exchanges, he left. We hastily called a meeting of the students and advised them of the Jewish Agency's response. Some students decided to go to Palestine anyway and were unfortunately captured by the British and interned on Cyprus. Following this incident, we received letters from our cousin in Palestine, Abraham Topiol, pleading with us not to come to Israel, because I would have a very difficult time trying to make a living there as a medical doctor.

From the beginning of my studies at the university, we tried to enrich ourselves culturally and started attending concerts and opera performances. Thanks to Esther's job at the American Joint Distribution Committee, she was able to get tickets at the American Red Cross Club and the PX store. When I was too busy studying to attend, I would ask friends to accompany Esther to concerts.

Esther and I were in love. She was working to support the family, while I was very busy trying to succeed in medical school, which required improving my fluency in the German language. She had to keep our social contacts with friends, since I was rarely available. We knew we wanted to get married, but we had to overcome the objections of my mother, who thought I was too young, and Esther's father, who did not think he should have any responsibility for his daughter who was still not married. We eventually married on June 11, 1946, at our home in Neu Freimann by an orthodox rabbi, as described by Esther in her memoirs. Our honeymoon occurred a year later, when we went to Bad Reichenhall, where Esther saw some small babies and decided that she wanted one for herself, despite the potential for difficulties.

She conceived very easily and was very happy. During the last three months of pregnancy, she developed severe dependent edema but was otherwise well. Unfortunately, though, the weather was hot, and it was difficult for her to work. Her father, who had remarried, was not perturbed in the slightest, and he made no effort to help her out financially, although he was doing very well dealing on the black market. The total disregard for his only child's welfare led to great difficulties between my parents and him. I, too, engaged in a few skirmishes with him. However, when he was ill and alone in Israel after his wife's death, I was the model son-in-law, going along with everything Esther wanted for him.

Eventually, my father persuaded Esther, who was under the care of Prof. Von Redwitz, my old mentor, to quit working. On August 14, 1948, she delivered our first child. I cannot describe the joy I experienced. He was a beautiful child.

We named the baby Marcel, after my friend Marcel Gheinic, who was a medical student from Romania who also lived in Neu Freimann. He had survived the war in the Soviet Union along with his parents and brother. He worked in various places. In order to survive in Russia one had to steal whatever products one could lay his hands on, and then barter those for other items, including food. Since he was too honest to steal he was mostly going around hungry. This made him more susceptible to infections. He developed pulmonary T.B. and tuberculous pericarditis, which then became restrictive to his heart function. He was often dyspneic on effort. When Esther became pregnant, he jokingly remarked that if the child were a boy, we should name him Marcel after him, since he would not live long. Unfortunately, Marcel Gheinic's dire predictions about his own premature death proved to be true. After we graduated from medical school together, I left for the U.S. and he remained in Germany. He decided to undergo surgery in Munich to free his heart from calcific pericarditis. I pleaded with him to come to New York, where I had arranged with Dr. Jerry Lord of Bellevue Hospital to operate on him. He stubbornly refused to come and wrote that he would come only when he felt well and was able to work. Unfortunately he died shortly after his operation in Munich.

We had a great deal of trouble deciding whether we should have our baby circumcised. After all many Jews who looked Aryan and might have gotten away with their lives perished because being circumcised gave them away. We finally decided that we would not give the Nazis and anti-Semites a victory over our feelings. Our Jewish custom would prevail.

Baby Marcel, who as a young man would change his name to the more American-sounding Michael, became ill with a respiratory infection at six months. He stared experiencing wheezing and mild dyspnea. I contacted a pediatric specialist from the university faculty, but his reaction was to pooh-pooh the whole thing until the baby's condition got much worse. There was no emergency room to go to, so I went with my friend Marcel to the doctor's home and asked him to come to examine the baby. When he refused, I got very angry. I told him that in the event that anything happened to my baby, I would act in the name of the many Jewish babies who had perished at the hands of the Nazis and that he would be held accountable. He got the message and came with us. His diagnosis was bronchiolitis. I don't remember what remedies he prescribed, except that I had to sit with the baby at the open window all through the night so he could breath the cool air. I also gave him inhalations of steam and an oral medication. No antibiotics were available to us at that time. But Marcel recovered and was a joy to our whole family.

# GETTING TO THE U.S.

Since emigrating to Palestine was out of the question, we turned our attentions to the U.S. When President Truman persuaded Congress to admit 100,000 refugees to the U.S., we applied and eventually were able to get our visas—not without difficulty. There were always vultures lurking all over, trying to make money of other people's misery.

We had to undergo a series of investigations and health screenings, in addition to guarantees from U.S. sponsors indicating that jobs awaited us upon arrival. My Aunt Sarah had guaranteed me a job as a buttonhole maker in her sweater shop. During my interview with a U.S. consular representative, I was questioned as to whether I was a communist before the war (at a tender age of 13½). When he realized how old I was, he sheepishly turned his questions to my job in the U.S. He asked whether he should believe that I wanted to work as a buttonhole maker when I was just graduated from medical school. I answered with my usual audacity that it would be a lie if I answered in the affirmative, and that I could not understand such a law. It apparently went over well with him and he promptly signed my papers.

The next hassle we had to overcome related to the physical examinations that we underwent at the Funk Kaserne in Munich. The routine was that one or two days after the physical examination, the names of people who passed would be posted on a bulletin board. We found all of our names except Sam's. That same day a macher vulture contacted my father and told him that Sam did not pass the examination, but for $3,000 he could arrange for Sam to pass.

The supposed reason for Sam's failure to pass was TB. Sam had tuberculosis osteomyelitis as a child, and it was arrested and cured. He had undergone a physical examination by Prof. Bergmann from the Faculty of Medicine, a very well respected doctor, just about three months before. This prior exam included a chest x-ray that was revealed no such illness. I found out that this macher was working with a German physician whom the American authorities had contracted to examine applicants for entry to the U.S. They were engaged in extortion of money from many people.

Since I did not have any money and to appeal to these people would be futile, I went to Prof. Bergmann's office and got the x-ray of Sam's chest. Then I went to see the German doctor at the Funk Kaserne, and introduced myself as Dr. Lederman. I informed him that I was aware of his extortionist practices and that I had a witness to that effect and showed him Sam's x-ray. I then told him that if he did not pass Sam, I would blow the lid off this scandalous affair. He was flabbergasted and guiltily agreed to pass Sam.

Soon after, we left for the U.S. We were still scared that the crooks might do something to prevent us from going. Even when we were safely aboard the ship, the Captain Ballou, in Bremerhaven, we were nervous. We saw other people being taken off the boat for one reason or another. I am still embarrassed that I did not expose that disgusting scam and instead let those vultures continue their nasty extortionist procedures. I was just too afraid of those people. It was a very dark period in human relations, and it seemed like anything could happen.

I tried to leave all those experiences behind me as I started my journey to the United States of America. I may someday summarize my life in the U.S.

Ezjel Lederman

*E*zjel Lederman never did write about his life in this country. He kept putting the task off for some future time, when his life would not be so busy. He lived a full and fulfilling life, enriched by his experiences as a husband, father, and healer. He took tremendous pride in his professional accomplishments, having earned the respect of his peers and the love and trust of innumerable patients. His children's accomplishments also filled him with love and pride. He died on February 27, 1995, at the age of 69. He will never be forgotten.

3454991